100 MATHS HOMEWORK

## RENEWED PRIMARY FRAMEWORK

# 100 MATHS HOMEWORK ACTIVITIES

## YEAR 2

Caroline Cliss[illegible] Cooper

## Credits

**Authors**
Caroline Clissold
Richard Cooper

**Development Editor**
Nicola Morgan

**Editor**
Ruth Burns

**Assistant Editor**
Margaret Eaton

**Illustrations**
Debbie Clark (Beehive Illustration)
Jenny Tulip (Beehive Illustration)

**Series Designer**
Helen Taylor

**Designer**
Macmillan Publishing Solutions

Designed using Adobe InDesign

Published by Scholastic Ltd
Villiers House
Clarendon Avenue
Leamington Spa
Warwickshire CV32 5PR

www.scholastic.co.uk

Printed by Bell and Bain Ltd, Glasgow

1 2 3 4 5 6 7 8 9 9 0 1 2 3 4 5 6 7 8

**British Library Cataloguing-in-Publication Data**
A catalogue record for this book is available from the British Library.

ISBN 978-1407-10217-7

# Contents

## About the series

*100 Maths Homework Activities* offers a complete solution to your planning and resourcing for maths homework activities. There are six books in the series, one for each year group from Year 1 to Year 6.

Each *100 Maths Homework Activities* book contains 72 homework activities, which cover the Renewed Framework objectives, and 36 puzzles and problems, which focus on the Using and applying objectives.

## About the homework activities

Each homework activity is presented as a photocopiable page, with some supporting notes for parents and carers provided underneath the activity.

Unit C1 Homework activity

Name Date

**Measures**

- Record the correct measurements on the lines below.

The string is ______ cm long.

The apples weigh ______ kg.

The bananas weigh just over ______ kg.

There is just over ______ litres of liquid in the jug.

There is just under ______ litres of liquid in the jug.

**Dear Helper**

Please help your child to read the scales to work out the answers. Encourage your child to write the answers in the spaces provided. If your child has difficulty, count along each scale with them in the appropriate intervals. For a challenge, encourage them to try to give an accurate reading.

SCHOLASTIC PHOTOCOPIABLE 100 MATHS HOMEWORK ACTIVITIES • YEAR 2 43

BLOCK C

Teachers' notes relating to the activities appear in grid format at the beginning of each block's activities. When exactly the homework is set and followed up is left to your professional judgement.

Across the *100 Maths Homework Activities* series, the homework activities cover a range of homework types. Some of the activities are for sharing. These encourage the child to discuss the homework task with a parent or carer, and may, for example, involve the home context, or a game to be played with the carer. Other activities involve investigations or problem-solving tasks. Again, the parent or carer is encouraged to participate in the activity, offering support to the child, and discussing the activity and its outcomes with the child.

## Using the homework activities

Each homework page includes a 'Helper note', which explains the aim of the homework and how the adult can support their child if he or she cannot get started. It is recommended that some form of homework diary be used alongside these activities, through which to establish an effective home-school dialogue about the children's enjoyment and understanding of the homework. A homework diary page is provided on page 6 of this book.

## Teachers' notes

The teachers' notes appear in a grid format at the start of each block's homework activities. Each grid contains the following information:

- the Framework unit
- the homework activity's title
- a brief description of the format and content of the activity, which will help you to decide which homework activity to choose
- the Renewed Framework learning objective/s
- a 'Managing the homework' section which provides two types of help – 'before' and 'after'. The 'before' notes provide suggestions for ways to introduce and explain the homework before the children take it home. These notes might include a brief oral activity to undertake as preparation for the homework. The 'after' notes provide suggestions for how to manage the review of the homework when the children return with it to school. Suggestions include discussing strategies used for solving a problem, comparing solutions, and playing a game as a class.

## About the puzzles and problems

The puzzles and problems (pages 90–107) provide coverage of the Using and applying mathematics objectives and can be used very flexibly to provide children with a comprehensive range of fun maths tasks to take home. The grid displayed on page 89 shows which puzzles and problems cover each of the Using and applying objectives.

Puzzles and problems

5 Puzzling pyramid

How many triangles can you find in this pyramid?

6 Let's play darts!

Kanika threw three darts.

More than one dart can go in each score.

What is the highest score Kanika could get?

Write all the scores Kanika could get if each dart hit a different number.



92 100 MATHS HOMEWORK ACTIVITIES • YEAR 2 SCHOLASTIC

The puzzles and problems are based on work that the children will be covering during the year and should test their skills at that level. Some of the questions may be solved quickly, others will require more thought. Either way, children should be encouraged to try a variety of different approaches to solving problems and to look for clues and patterns in maths. It is essential for them to read the question carefully (sometimes more than once) to understand exactly what they are being asked to do. A few of the puzzles and problems will require an everyday household item or the help of a family member. Most should be readily solved by a child working on their own.

Remind the children that if a problem or puzzle is proving too difficult or frustrating, they could leave it and come back to it later with a refreshed mind!

## Developing a homework policy

The homework activities have been written with the DCSF 'Homework guidelines' in mind. These can be located in detail on the Standards website **www.standards.dfes.gov.uk/homework/goodpractice** The guidelines are a good starting point for planning an effective homework policy. Effective home-school partnerships are also vital in ensuring a successful homework policy.

## Encouraging home-school links

An effective working partnership between teachers and parents and carers makes a positive impact upon children's attainment in mathematics. The homework activities in this book are part of that partnership. Parents and carers are given guidance on what the homework is about, and on how to be involved with the activity. There are suggestions for helping the children who are struggling with a particular concept, such as ways of counting on or back mentally, and extension ideas for children who would benefit from slightly more advanced work.

The homework that is set across the curriculum areas for Year 2 should amount to a total of about one hour per week. The homework diary page, which can be sent home with the homework activity with opportunities for a response from the parents/carers, can be found on page 6 of this book.

## Using the activities with *100 Maths Framework Lessons Year 2*

The activities covered in this book fit the planning within the book *100 Maths Framework Lessons Year 2* (also published by Scholastic Ltd). As teachers plan their work on a week-by-week basis, so the homework activities can be chosen to fit the appropriate unit of work.

# Homework diary

| Name of activity & date sent home | Child's comments | | Helper's comments | Teacher's comments |
|---|---|---|---|---|
| | Did you like this activity? Draw a face. ☺ a lot 😐 a little ☹ not much | How much did you learn? Draw a face. ☺ a lot 😐 a little ☹ not much | | |
| | | | | |
| | | | | |
| | | | | |

# Counting, partitioning and calculating



| Activity | Learning objectives | Managing the homework |
|---|---|---|
| **A1** | | |
| **Number line**<br>Make sequences of numbers by writing a two-digit number on a number line, then completing the sequence. | Read and write two-digit numbers; extend number sequences | **Before:** Tell the children that they will be practising sequencing work.<br>**After:** Review the activity, inviting children to demonstrate their work. |
| **Combining cards**<br>Use partitioning cards to mentally combine and write the number sentence. | Read and write two-digit and three-digit numbers | **Before:** Explain that the children will be practising combining tens and ones.<br>**After:** Review the activity, inviting children to demonstrate their work. Hold up two- and three-digit numbers and ask them to write number sentences. |
| **Dots before your eyes**<br>Practise counting by grouping. | Count up to 100 objects by grouping them and counting in tens, fives or twos | **Before:** Demonstrate how to group and count items on the board.<br>**After:** Ask some of the children to demonstrate what they did, using an OHT of the homework sheet. Ask: *When is it best to group things into tens when we count them? Why? When we haven't got a group of 10, what other groups could we use?* |
| **Fill your ladder**<br>Generate two-digit numbers and order these from lowest to highest. | Order two-digit numbers | **Before:** Model this game. When you make each two-digit number, show both possibilities and ask which would be best. For example: *Which would fit best – 34 or 43?* It may not matter at first, but as the rungs fill up it will. Show the children how the numbers are ordered from smallest to biggest.<br>**After:** Revisit the game as a whole-class activity. |
| **A2** | | |
| **In the bin**<br>A game of counting in twos. | Read and write two-digit and three-digit numbers; extend number sequences | **Before:** Explain that the children will be playing a game to practise counting in twos.<br>**After:** Write a number on the board. Ask the children to tell you the next four numbers that come after it if they count in twos. Ask for some numbers that come before it. Repeat with a higher number. |
| **Totals to 10**<br>Add three small numbers, two of which should total 10. Explain the addition strategy to a helper. | Add mentally a single-digit number or a multiple of 10 to any two-digit number | **Before:** Explain that the children will be practising to add three numbers using the strategy of finding two that make 10 first.<br>**After:** Invite the children to tell everyone the highest/lowest/most numbers they found. Ask the children which pairs total 10 or a multiple of 10. Establish that adding 10 to a number is easier than adding on other numbers. |
| **Stepping stones**<br>Count on and back in steps of 3, 4 and 5. | Read and write two-digit numbers; describe and extend number sequences | **Before:** Explain to the children that they will be practising counting in threes, fours and fives. Fill in the step number and a few numbers on each line to show the children what steps you want them to count in and the number range.<br>**After:** Repeat the activity with the class using an OHT of the sheet. |
| **Snaky stripes**<br>Count back in steps of 3, 4 and 5. | Read and write two-digit numbers; describe and extend number sequences | **Before:** Write appropriate step sizes and start numbers for each ability group as in the example. You may wish to give additional number clues in some cases.<br>**After:** Using an OHT of the sheet, invite some children to share their work. Ask the other children whether the number lines are correct and how they know. |

## Counting, partitioning and calculating

| Activity | Learning objectives | Managing the homework |
|---|---|---|
| **A3** | | |
| **Arrow sentences**<br>Write number sentences. | Use the symbols +, –, ×, ÷ and = to record and interpret number sentences involving all four operations; calculate the value of an unknown in a number sentence (for example, 30 - ? = 24, ? ÷ 2 = 6) | **Before:** Explain that the children will need to choose numbers to make addition and subtraction arrow sentences. You will need to write numbers in the boxes for each child/ability group.<br>**After:** Review, asking the children to give examples of their work. Write ? + ? = 10 + 2 on the board and ask for possible answers. |
| **Odds and evens**<br>An odds-and-evens game. | Read and write two-digit and three-digit numbers in figures and words; recognise odd and even numbers | **Before:** Play the game with the children as a whole class to show them what to do.<br>**After:** Spin some pairs of numbers. Ask the children if they are odd or even. Total each pair and ask if the answer is odd or even. Bring to their attention the fact that when adding two odd numbers or two even numbers the answer is even. |
| **Opposites**<br>Matching card game for inversions. | Understand that subtraction is the inverse of addition and vice versa; use this to derive and record related addition and subtraction number sentences | **Before:** Demonstrate exactly what to do using enlarged cards from a copy of the homework sheet.<br>**After:** Play the game as a class. Put an addition sentence on the board. Ask: *What other addition can be made? What two subtractions can be made?* |
| **Split the number**<br>Use the partitioning method to add two two-digit numbers. | • Read and write two-digit and three-digit numbers in figures and words; use practical and informal methods to add and subtract two-digit numbers<br>• Partition two-digit numbers in different ways, including into multiples of 10 and 1 | **Before:** Make differentiated versions of the worksheet by filling in the four remaining numbers on the sheet. Demonstrate how to complete the activity.<br>**After:** Invite children to demonstrate some of their work. Ask questions such as: *Which number did you choose to partition? Why? How did you find your answer?* |

Name Date

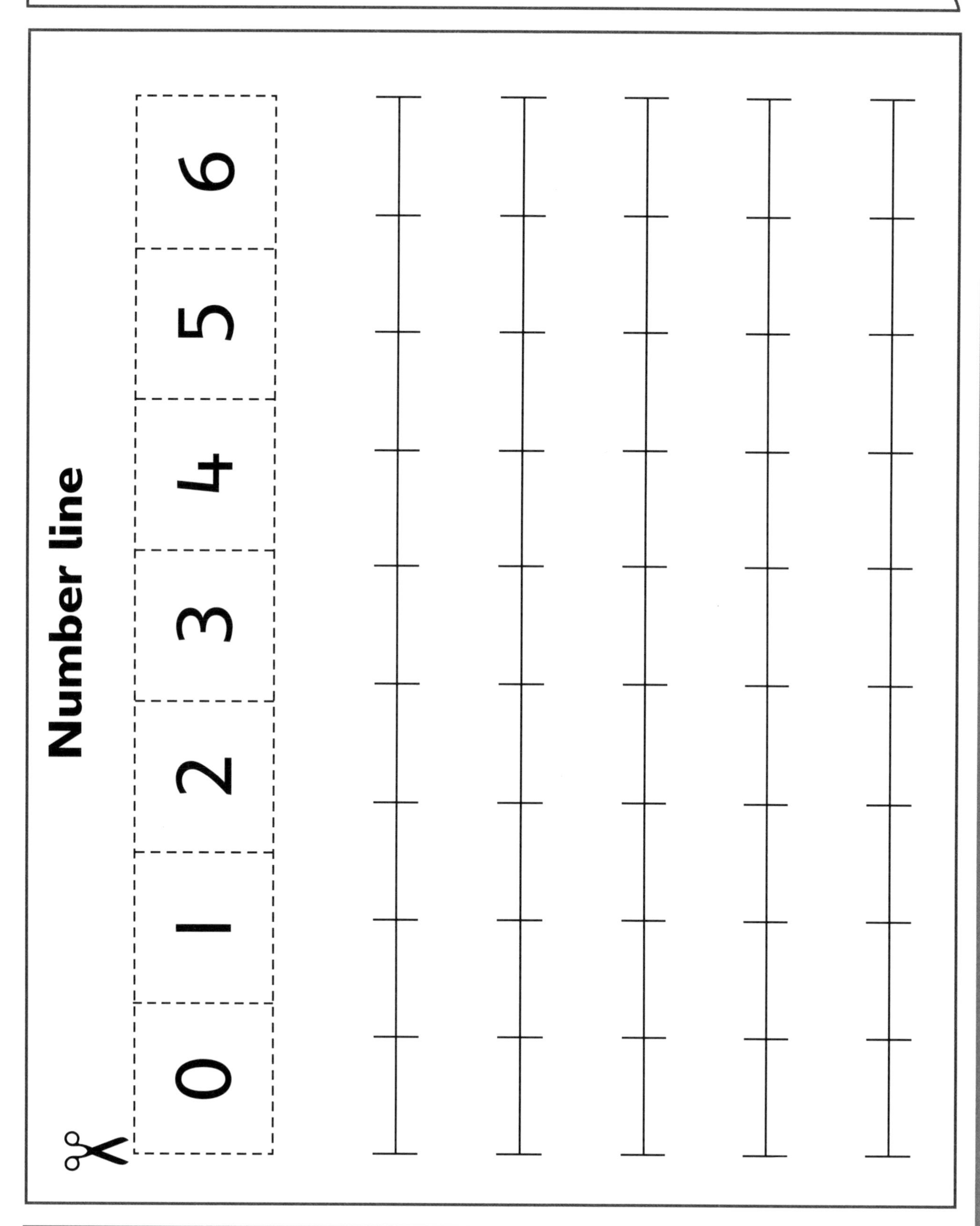


**Dear Helper**

This activity will help your child to read and write two-digit numbers and to extend sequences. Help your child to cut out the small number cards, then ask them to pick two cards and put them together to make a two-digit number (for example, 3 and 2 to make 32). Write the number in the middle of the number line. Ask your child to fill in the rest of the number line, counting up and down in ones from that number. If your child finds this difficult, write a two-digit number at the beginning of the number line, then ask them to count up from that number. If your child wants a challenge, ask them to count on and back in twos.

Name Date

# Combining cards

- Put the tens and ones cards together to make as many new numbers as you can. Record your work. For example:

| 40 | 1 | 41 |
|---|---|---|

40 + 1 = 41

| 5 | 2 |
|---|---|
| 7 | 1 |
| 40 | 10 |
| 70 | 30 |

**Dear Helper**
This activity will support the work that your child has been doing on partitioning. Help them to cut out the partitioning cards. Invite them to put one ten and one unit card together to make a new number (for example, 40 and 1 to make 41). Challenge them to make as many different two-digit numbers as they can, using different combinations of cards. Encourage them to record their work (for example, 40 + 1 = 41). If they need a challenge, ask them to make hundreds cards as well.

 

Name Date



# Dots before your eyes

- Count these dots by drawing hoops around each group of 10.

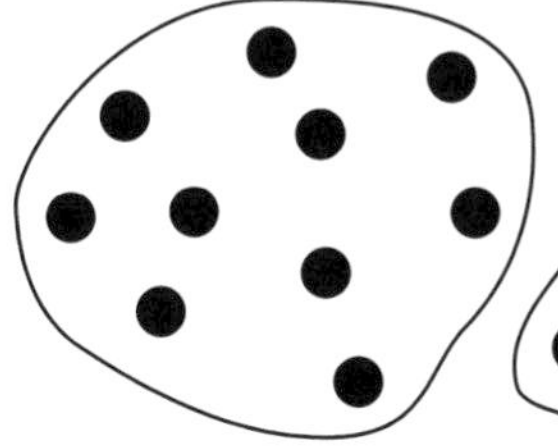

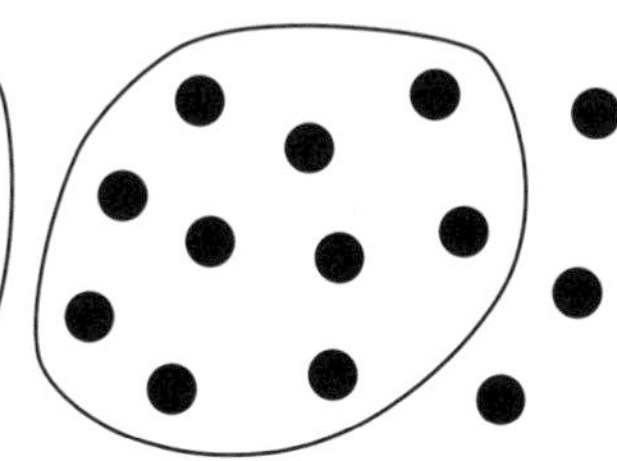

How many dots are there?

35

- Count these dots by drawing hoops around each group of 10.

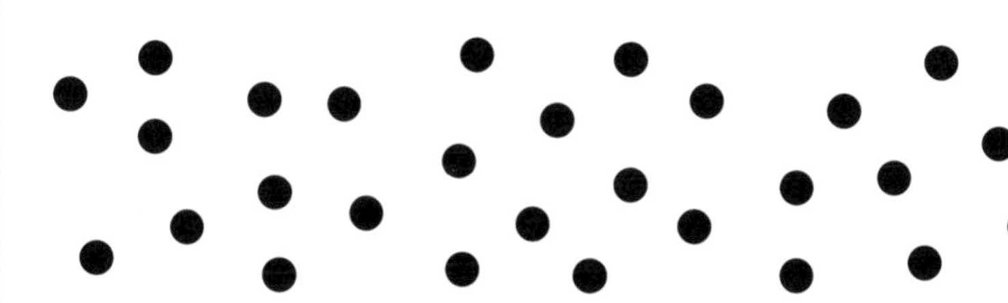

How many dots are there?

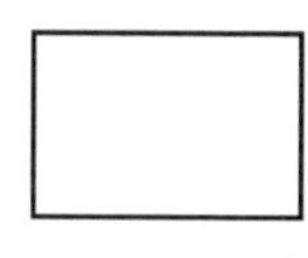

- Count these dots by drawing hoops around each group of 5.

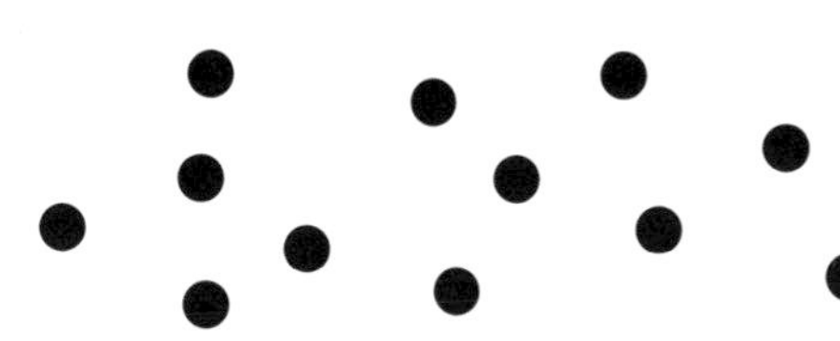

How many dots are there?

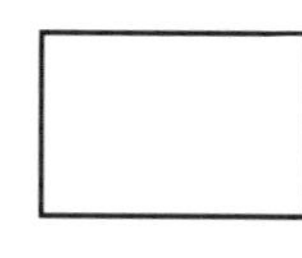

- Count these dots by drawing hoops around each group of 2.

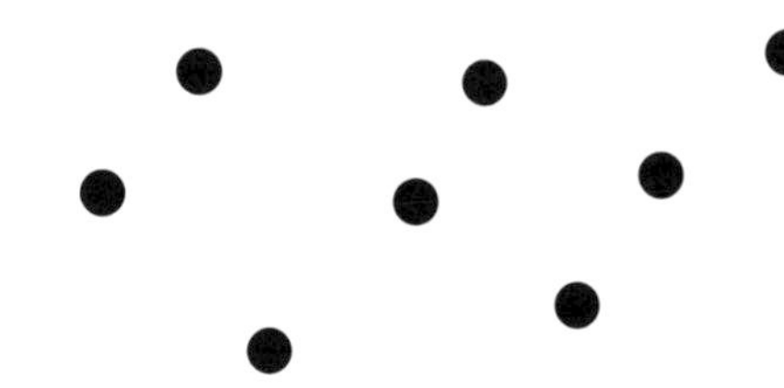

How many dots are there?

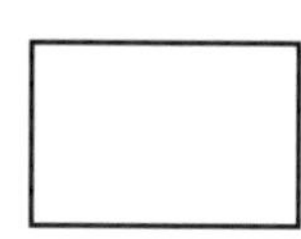

**Dear Helper**

This activity encourages your child to group numbers in order to help them count more efficiently. Read the instructions for counting each set of dots, then encourage your child to fill in the correct totals in the boxes. The first example has been done for you. If your child has difficulty, encourage them to mark dots as they count and then loop them together. For a challenge, ask your child to draw 12 dots on the back of the sheet and find all the possible ways of grouping.

Name Date

# Fill your ladder

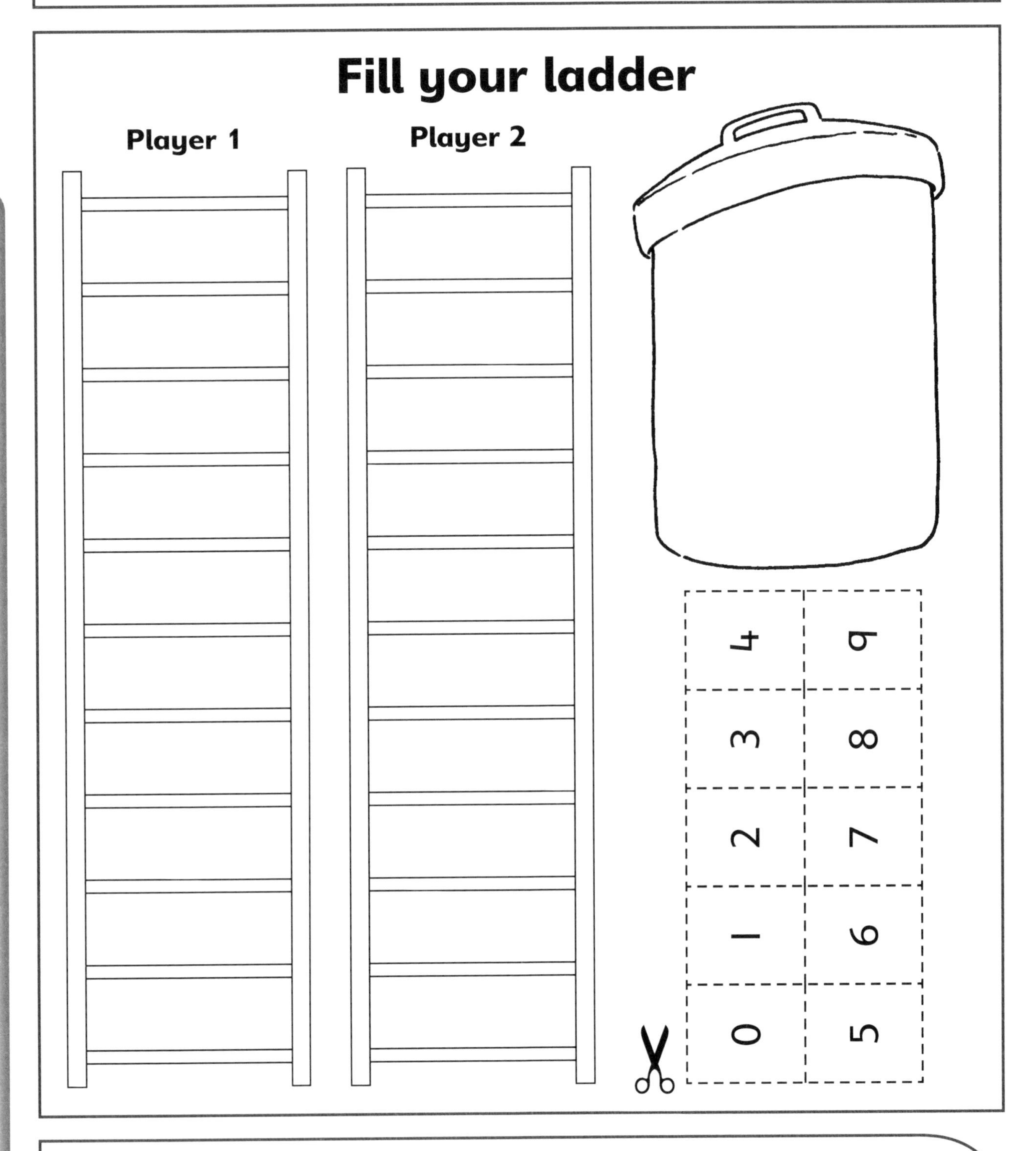


**Dear Helper**

This game will help your child to practise ordering numbers up to 100. Cut out the 0–9 number cards. The first player should choose two cards to make a two-digit number. Depending on whether the number is high or low, the player should write that number on an appropriate rung on their ladder. For example, a 4 and a 9 could make 49 or 94. They can choose to write 49 in the middle of the ladder, or 94 at the top. Remind the player that there are only ten rungs, so they need to choose their rung carefully. The next player should then take their turn. Choose which way around to use the numbers depending on the space left on the ladder. As the rungs fill up, a number may not fit on. When this happens tell the player to write that number in the 'bin' and let the next player take their turn. The winner is the first player to fill their ladder. If your child has difficulty, make numbers to 20 by choosing the 1 or the 2 as the tens number. For a challenge, encourage them to make a new 20 rung ladder and order all the numbers you both made onto it.

 

Name Date



# In the bin

Bin

| 0 | 1 | 2 | 3 | 4 | 5 | 6 | 7 | 8 | 9 |
|---|---|---|---|---|---|---|---|---|---|
| 0 | 1 | 2 | 3 | 4 | 5 | 6 | 7 | 8 | 9 |

**Dear Helper**

This game will help your child to count in twos. Cut out the number cards and place them face down. Player 1 takes two cards to make a two-digit start number which he/she then writes in the first box on the blank grid. Player 2 then takes two cards. If the two cards make a number that could follow the sequence of counting in twos from the start number, Player 2 writes this in the correct position on the grid and scores one point. If a number cannot be made in the sequence, it should be written in the 'bin'. For numbers that fit the sequence but do not fit on the grid, players should write this number on a separate piece of paper and award themselves a point. When the number grid has been completed, the player with the most points is the winner. If your child is having difficulty, make the first number a single-digit number. If they would like a challenge, ask them to make three-digit numbers.

BLOCK A

Name Date

# Totals to 10

- Choose three numbers from the selection shown below to add together. Make sure that two of the numbers you have chosen total 10 and add these together first.
- Next, add on the third number. Explain your work to your Helper.

| 2 | 3 | 4 | 6 | 7 | 8 |
|---|---|---|---|---|---|
| 12 | 13 | 14 | 16 | 17 | 18 |

| Numbers chosen: | Numbers totalling 10: | Addition: |
|---|---|---|
| 3 7 12 | 3 and 7 | 3 + 7 = 10<br>12 + 10 = 22 |
| | | |
| | | |
| | | |
| | | |

- Now make up some more similar sums on the back of this sheet.

**Dear Helper**

Your child has been learning how to look for numbers that total 10. Encourage them to explain their strategy to you. Now encourage them to use the strategy to add three numbers from the top of the page. If your child has difficulty, tell them to add the single digits only. If they would like a challenge, ask them to add the two-digit numbers only.

Name Date

# Stepping stones

| Step | | | | | | | | | | | |
|---|---|---|---|---|---|---|---|---|---|---|---|
| Step 3 | 3 | 6 | 9 | 12 | 15 | 18 | 21 | 24 | 27 | 30 | 33 |
| Step | | | | | | | | | | | |
| Step | | | | | | | | | | | |
| Step | | | | | | | | | | | |
| Step | | | | | | | | | | | |
| Step | | | | | | | | | | | |
| Step | | | | | | | | | | | |

**Dear Helper**

Your child has been learning to count in steps of 3, 4 and 5, from and back to small numbers. Encourage your child to look at the starting numbers and the step numbers that have already been filled in, and then to complete the number lines counting in steps of that number. The starting numbers and step numbers have been filled in according to your child's ability. An example has been done for you.

Name Date

# Snaky stripes

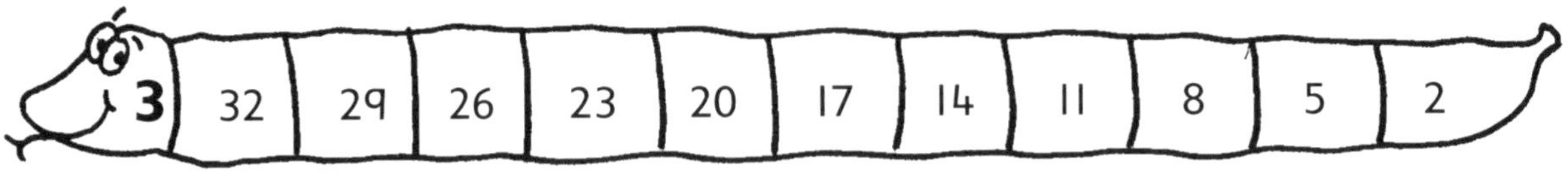

| 3 | 32 | 29 | 26 | 23 | 20 | 17 | 14 | 11 | 8 | 5 | 2 |
|---|---|---|---|---|---|---|---|---|---|---|---|

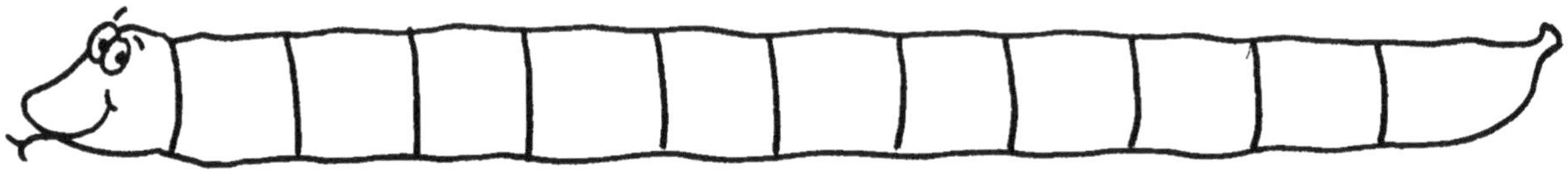

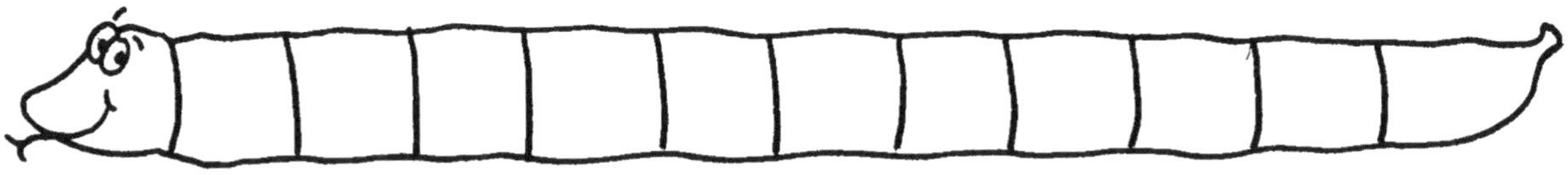

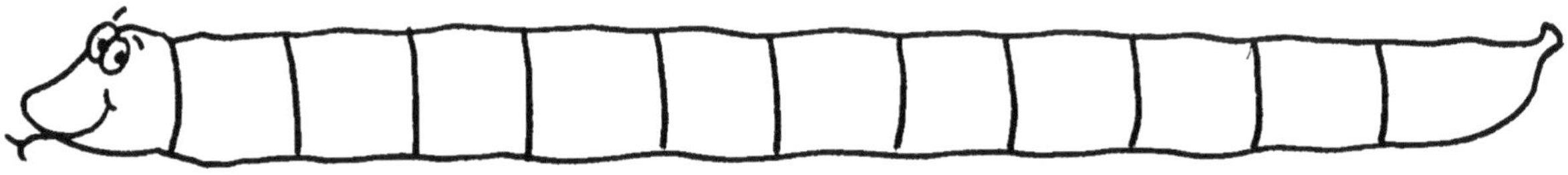

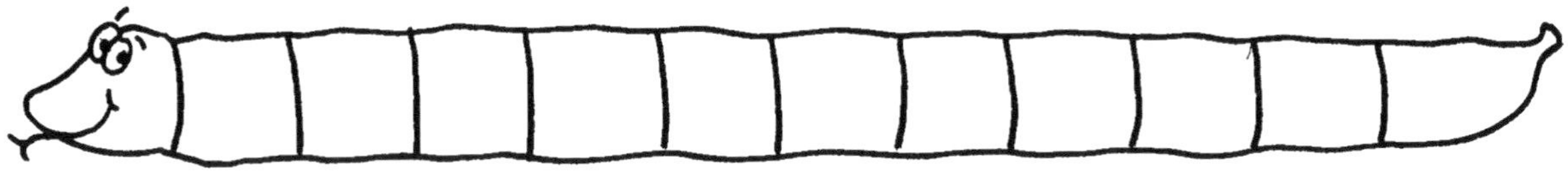

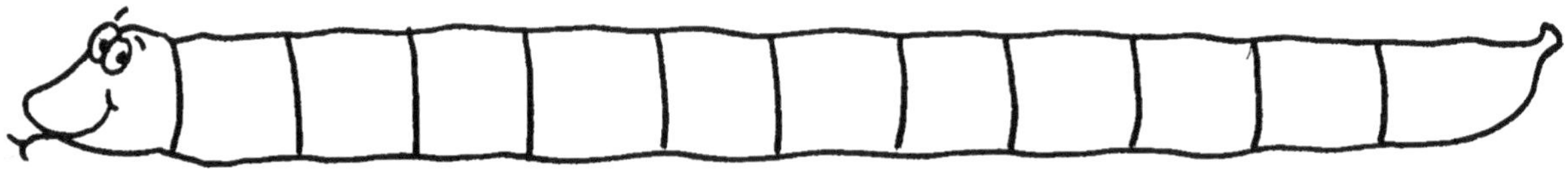

**Dear Helper**

Your child has been learning to count on and back in steps of 3, 4 and 5. In this activity, please focus on counting back. Your child's teacher has filled in a step size and start number on each snake. Encourage your child to complete each snake by counting back in steps of the numbers given. The first example has been done for you.

Name Date

# Arrow sentences

- Choose two numbers and make an arrow sentence.
  - One example has already been done for you.

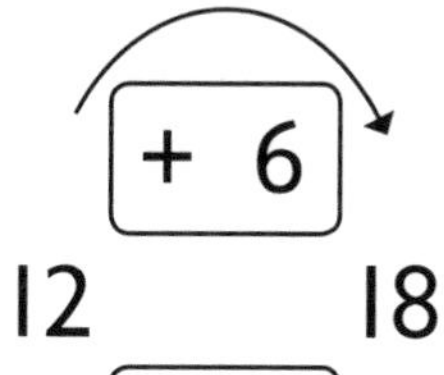

12 18

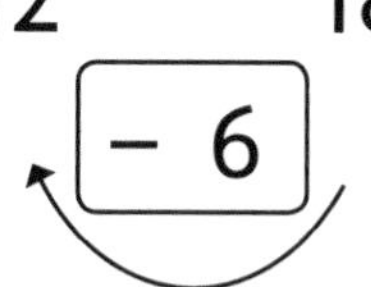

12 + 6 = 18

18 – 6 = 12

\+

–

\+ =

– =

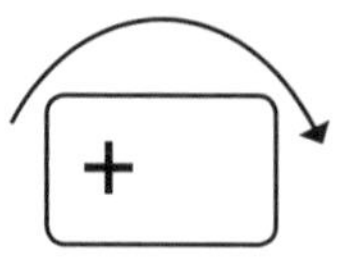

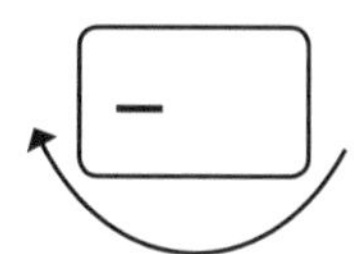

\+ =

– =

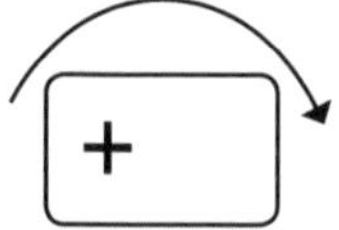

–

\+ =

– =

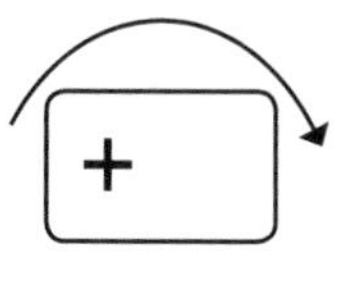

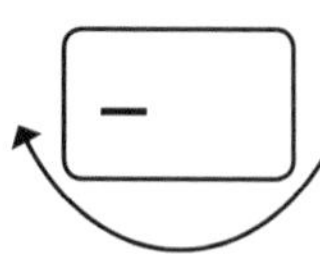

\+ =

– =

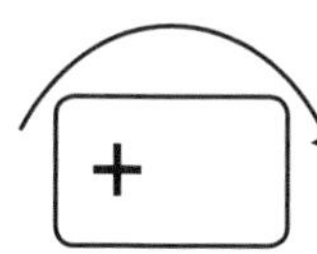

\+ =

– =

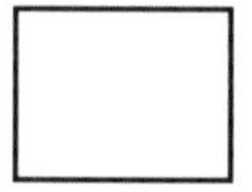   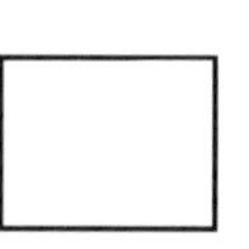 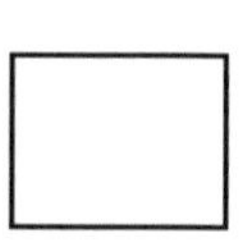 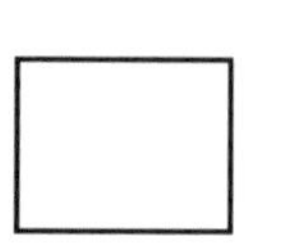 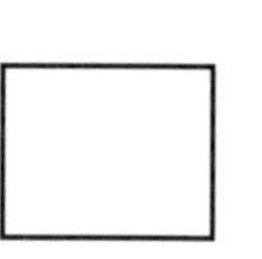 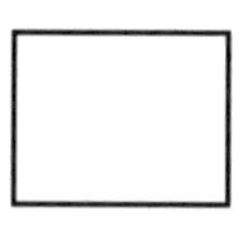

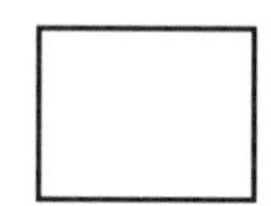 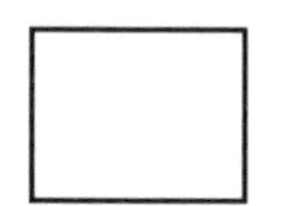   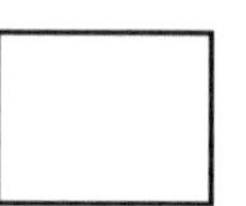 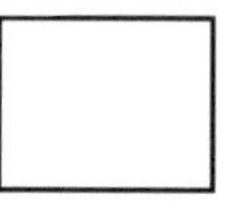 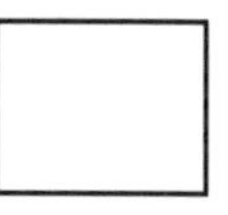 

**Dear Helper**

This activity will help to reinforce your child's mental addition and subtraction skills. The numbers in the boxes above have been chosen specifically for them. Encourage your child to choose two numbers for each arrow sentence, then help them to complete each arrow sentence by working out and writing down which number they will need to add and subtract each time.

Name Date

# Odds and evens

**Dear Helper**

This game will help your child to recognise odd and even numbers. You will each need a counter to place on Start. Cut out the spinners. Take turns to spin a number on each spinner (use a paper clip and pencil to do this, as shown in the illustration above). Add the two numbers together. If the total is odd, move on to the next white circle. If it is even, move on to the next black circle. The first player to reach Finish is the winner. If your child has difficulty, use one spinner only and identify whether the number landed on is odd or even. For a challenge, spin the two-digit spinner twice and add those numbers.

Name Date

# Opposites

| $3 + 2 = 5$ | $5 - 2 = 3$ |
|---|---|
| $5 + 10 = 15$ | $15 - 10 = 5$ |
| $14 + 5 = 19$ | $19 - 5 = 14$ |
| $11 + 10 = 21$ | $21 - 10 = 11$ |
| $13 + 12 = 25$ | $25 - 12 = 13$ |
| $15 + 20 = 35$ | $35 - 20 = 15$ |
| $16 + 30 = 46$ | $46 - 30 = 16$ |
| $20 + 23 = 43$ | $43 - 23 = 20$ |
| $24 + 35 = 59$ | $59 - 35 = 24$ |
| $26 + 32 = 58$ | $58 - 32 = 26$ |

**Dear Helper**

Your child been learning that addition is the opposite of subtraction and that they can work out the answers to subtraction calculations from knowing the matching additions. Help your child to cut out the cards then jumble them up to play a matching game. See how long it takes your child to match each addition with its matching subtraction.

BLOCK A

Name Date

# Split the number

- Choose two numbers to add together using the partitioning method.
  - Remember to keep your biggest number whole and partition the smaller number into tens and units.

| 15 | 23 |  | 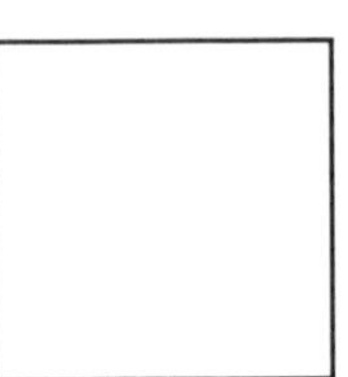 |  |  |
|---|---|---|---|---|---|

For example:

| Numbers chosen: | Partitioning: | My answer is: |
|---|---|---|
| 15 and 23 | 23 + 10 + 5 = 33 + 5 | 38 |
| Numbers chosen: | Partitioning: | My answer is: |
| Numbers chosen: | Partitioning: | My answer is: |
| Numbers chosen: | Partitioning: | My answer is: |
| Numbers chosen: | Partitioning: | My answer is: |

- Now make up some more sums, using the partitioning method, on the back of this sheet.

**Dear Helper**
Your child has been learning how to add two numbers by keeping the biggest number whole and partitioning the other number into tens and units before adding them together. For example, 23 + 12 = 23 + 10 + 2 = 33 + 2 = 35. The numbers have been specially chosen for your child's ability level. Ask them to explain the strategy to you before beginning the activity.

# Securing number facts, understanding shape

| Activity | Learning objectives | Managing the homework |
|---|---|---|
| **B1** | | |
| **Toy shopping**<br>Use a range of coins to make different totals. | Solve problems involving addition in the context of pounds and pence | **Before:** Tell the children that they will be practising work in money values and coins.<br>**After:** Review the activity, asking some of the children to show examples of their work. |
| **How much?**<br>Share a shopping activity. | Solve problems involving addition and subtraction in the context of pounds and pence | **Before:** Tell the children that they will be playing a shopping game that involves totalling prices and giving change.<br>**After:** Review the activity. Ask questions such as: *I have £1. I buy something and am given one coin as change. How much could I have spent?* |
| **Describe me**<br>Describe the properties of shapes. | Visualise common 2D shapes; identify shapes from pictures of them in different positions and orientations; sort and describe shapes, referring to their properties | **Before:** Tell the children that they will be looking at properties of shapes and describing them.<br>**After:** Review the activity. Describe the properties of some shapes and ask the children to tell you what they are. |
| **Double trouble maze**<br>Children have to find their way through a doubling maze. | Derive and recall doubles of all numbers to 20. | **Before:** Demonstrate how to go around the maze by correctly doubling the number at each junction.<br>**After:** Copy a correctly completed maze onto an OHT, and work through it with the class. |
| **Which coins?**<br>Make up amounts with a £1 or £2 coin and one or two others and record the totals as number sentences (for example, £1 + 20p + 2p = £1.22). | Solve problems involving addition in the context of pounds and pence | **Before:** Fill in appropriate numbers on the worksheet according to the children's ability.<br>**After:** Ask some children to explain what they did, using examples from their work. Ask questions such as: *How did you know that was the least number of coins? If there hadn't been a 20p coin, what else could you have used?* Find out whether they were able to do this homework independently. |
| **DJ Peejay**<br>Match calculations and answers. | Derive and recall multiplication facts for the 2-, 5- and 10-times tables and the related division facts; recognise multiples of 2, 5 and 10 | **Before:** Recite the 2-, 5- and 10-times tables with the class.<br>**After:** Have a written speed test on the work covered by the sheet. |
| **B2** | | |
| **The name game**<br>Make up numbers from a selection of digit cards and record them as words and numerals. | Read and write two-digit and three-digit numbers in figures and words | **Before:** Tell the children that they will be practising naming numbers.<br>**After:** Review the activity, inviting children to tell everyone the highest/lowest/how many numbers they found. |
| **Get some help!**<br>Children make up word problems for their helper to answer. | Solve problems involving addition and subtraction | **Before:** Explain that this homework needs to be done with a helper. Demonstrate making up word problems using the information given.<br>**After:** Ask the children to share their problems and talk about the different ways that they and their helper solved them. |
| **Beat the clock!**<br>In a timed activity, children complete number sentences using + and -. | Derive and recall all addition and subtraction facts for each number to at least 10 | **Before:** Tell the children that they will be practising addition and subtraction facts to at least 10, and that they will be timed to see how quickly they can recall these facts.<br>**After:** Select volunteers for a speed challenge, where you call out the part of the fact and the children call out or write the missing part. |

BLOCK B

| Activity | Learning objectives | Managing the homework |
|---|---|---|
| **Shape puzzle**<br>Children complete a puzzle based on values of shapes. | Describe patterns and relationships involving numbers or shapes; make predictions and test these with examples | **Before:** Decide which values you want the shapes to have, filling in enough of the totals to make the puzzle possible to solve. Differentiate the activity by varying the values of the shapes.<br>**After:** Using an OHT of the sheet, ask the children to describe how they solved the puzzle. Ask questions such as: *Which row or column did you look at first? Why?* |
| **Give us a clue!**<br>A shape-matching game. | Visualise common 2D shapes and 3D solids; identify shapes from pictures of them in different positions and orientations; sort and describe shapes, referring to their properties | **Before:** Show the homework page and go through several examples.<br>**After:** Review the homework, asking the children to share their answers. Give other clues for these shapes to check that they know the important properties. Give clues that could be applicable to two shapes and ask the difference between them. |
| **Reflective symmetry**<br>Draw lines of symmetry on letters of the alphabet. | Identify reflective symmetry in patterns and 2D shapes and draw lines of symmetry in shapes | **Before:** Show examples of reflective symmetry to the class.<br>**After:** Ask the children to point out examples of reflective symmetry around the classroom. |
| **B3** | | |
| **Rounding up**<br>Estimate answers to addition calculations before working them out. | • Use knowledge of number facts and operations to estimate and check answers to calculations<br>• Describe patterns and relationships involving numbers or shapes, make predictions and test these with examples<br>• Solve problems involving addition, subtraction, multiplication or division | **Before:** Differentiate the activity by varying the numbers in the boxes at the top of the page. Work through examples together, encouraging the children to estimate by rounding.<br>**After:** Ask the children to give examples of their work. Discuss rounding each number to a multiple of 10 and adding them to give a basic estimate. Discuss the strategies they used to total the numbers. |
| **Making problems**<br>Make up problems for a helper to answer. | Solve problems involving addition, subtraction, multiplication or division in contexts of numbers and pounds and pence | **Before:** Explain that this homework needs to be done with a helper. Demonstrate how to make up problems using the information.<br>**After:** Invite the children to share the problems they made up and to talk about the ways that they and their helper solved them. |
| **Right or wrong?**<br>Decide whether general statements about numbers and shapes are right or wrong. | Describe patterns and relationships involving numbers or shapes, make predictions and test these with examples | **Before:** Explain that the children need to work out whether the statements on the sheet are right or wrong and then write down their reason(s). Everyone should be able to do the first two examples. More able children may also like to try the last one.<br>**After:** Discuss each statement, inviting the children to give as many reasons as possible for their answers. |
| **What a problem!**<br>Children complete problem-solving questions based on money. | Solve problems involving addition, subtraction, multiplication or division in contexts of numbers, measures or pounds and pence | **Before:** Differentiate the sheets by filling in amounts of money appropriate to each child/ability group.<br>**After:** Check the children's work with them. Ask how they worked out their solutions. Which strategies did they use to work out the change – for example, did they count on? |
| **Doubles and halves**<br>Practise doubling and halving. | Understand that halving is the inverse of doubling and derive and recall doubles of all numbers to 20, and the corresponding halves | **Before:** Differentiate the activity by filling in appropriate numbers on the sheet.<br>**After:** Ask the children to explain what they did. Ask questions such as: *How did you double a number? Did you know the answer, or did you partition, or did you count on?* Find out whether they were able to do the homework independently. |
| **You are the teacher!**<br>Check the answers to addition and subtraction calculations. | Use knowledge of number facts and operations to estimate and check answers to calculations | **Before:** Talk about the importance of checking answers to calculations.<br>**After:** Next time you have a short written test, ask the children to swap their papers with a partner and mark each others' work. |

Name Date

# Toy shopping

25p I used:
20p and 5p

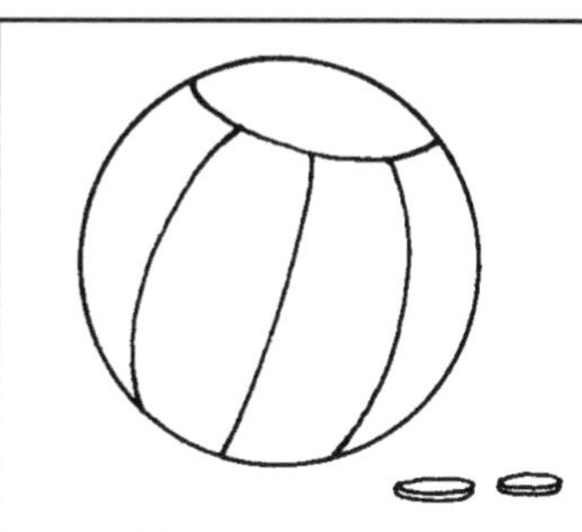

11p I used:

30p I used:

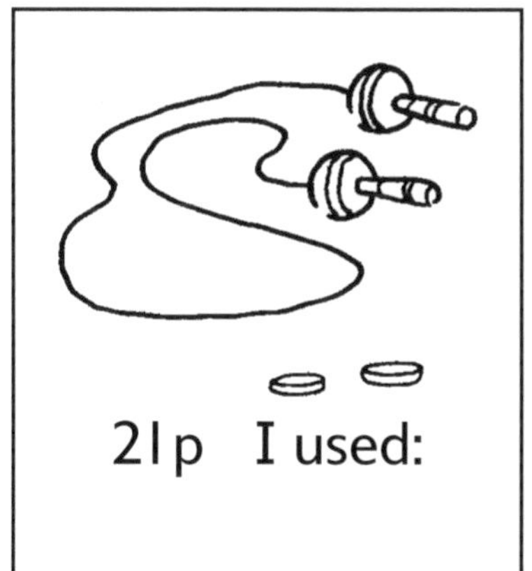

21p I used:

32p I used:

26p I used:

28p I used:

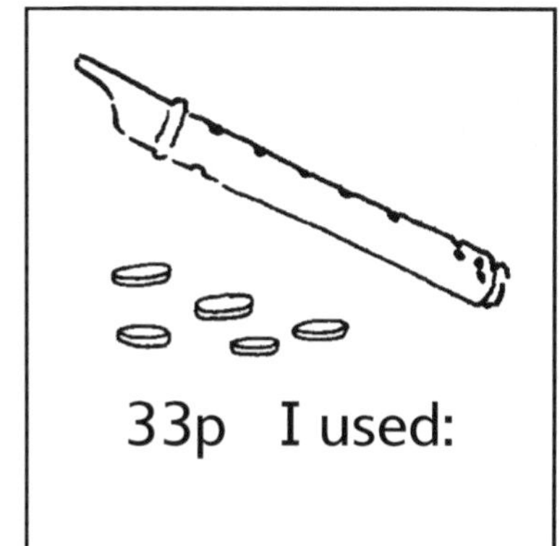

33p I used:

42p I used:

**Dear Helper**
This activity will provide opportunities for your child to practise their coin work. Provide your child with several 1p, 2p, 5p, 10p and 20p coins. Ask your child to look at the price underneath each toy and put the correct coins onto each picture to make up the price of the toy. Challenge them to use the fewest coins possible to make up the price, and to tell you what they are doing. Encourage them to record which coins they used. The first example has been done for you.

Name Date

# How much?

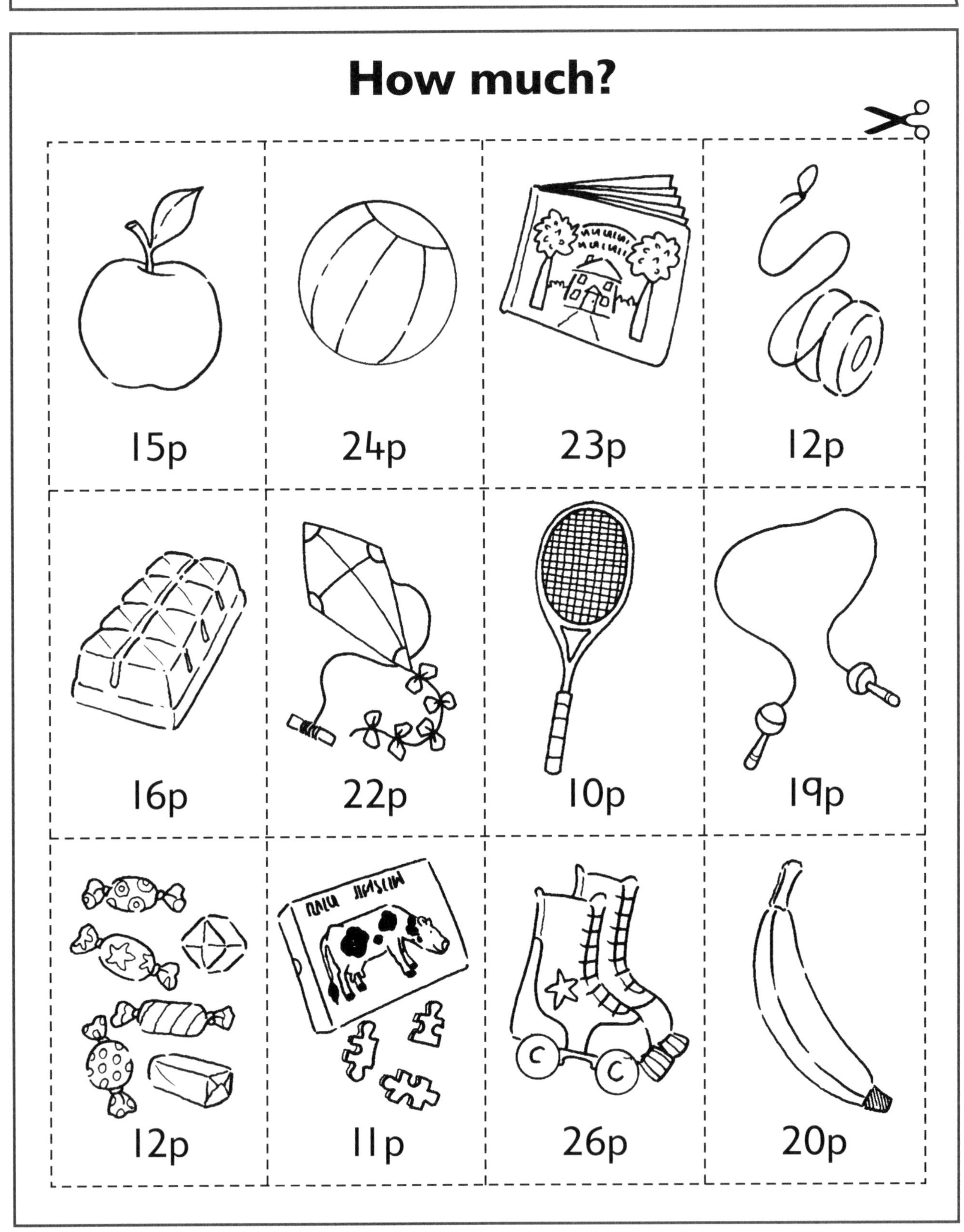


**Dear Helper**
This activity provides practice in working out totals and giving change. Cut out the cards and provide your child with several 1p, 2p, 5p, 10p, 20p and 50p coins. You can both take turns to be shopper and shopkeeper. The shopper should choose two cards and give them to the shopkeeper together with 50p. The shopkeeper should work out the total cost of the two items, and give the shopper their change. If your child has difficulty, use one card and 30p. For more of a challenge, use three cards and £1.

Name Date

# Describe me

### 1. Description

Sides: ______________

Corners: ______________

Symmetrical: ______

Name: ______________________________

### 2. Description

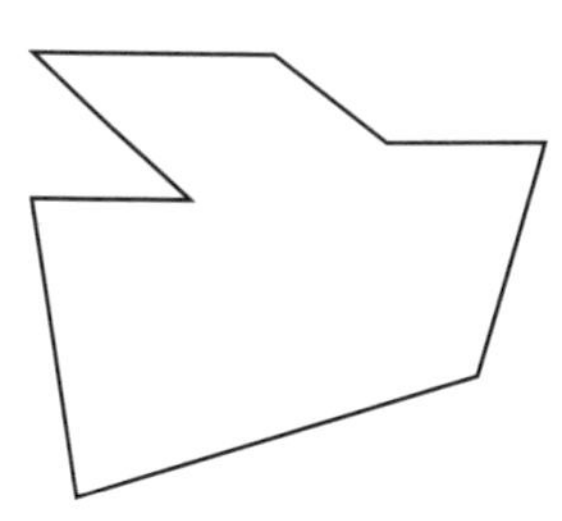

Sides: ______________

Corners: ______________

Symmetrical: ______

Name: ______________________________

### 3. Description

Sides: ______________

Corners: ______________

Symmetrical: ______

Name: ______________________________

### 4. Description

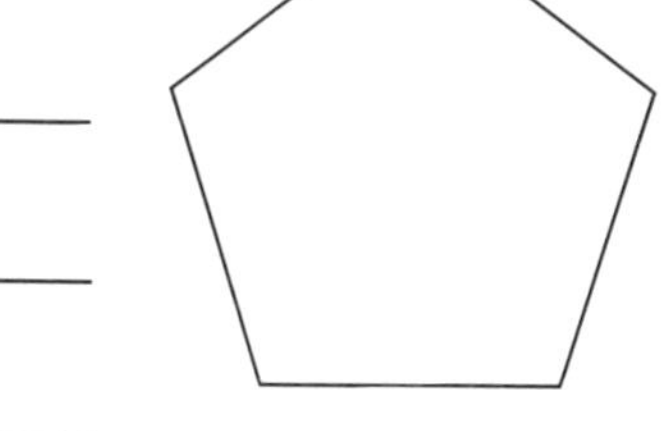

Sides: ______________

Corners: ______________

Symmetrical: ______

Name: ______________________________

### 5. Description

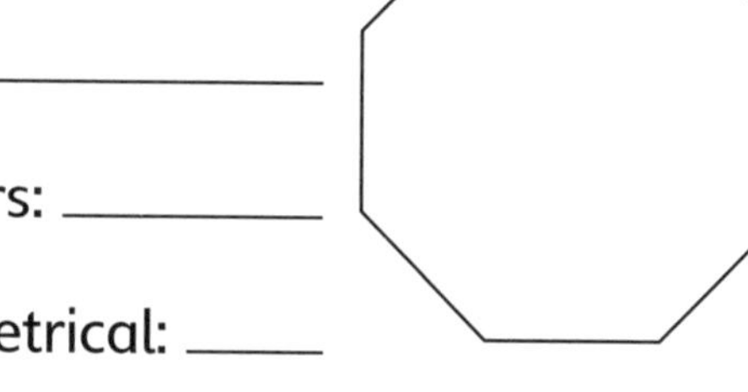

Sides: ______________

Corners: ______________

Symmetrical: ______

Name: ______________________________

### 6. Description

Sides: ______________

Corners: ______________

Symmetrical: ______

Name: ______________________________

**Dear Helper**

This activity will reinforce work on properties of different shapes. Invite your child to talk about each shape in turn. Encourage them to fill in all the spaces. Give prompts and write the name of the shape if your child is having difficulty. If they need a challenge, ask them to focus on two shapes that have the same name and note their similarities and differences.

BLOCK B

Name Date

BLOCK B

# Double trouble maze

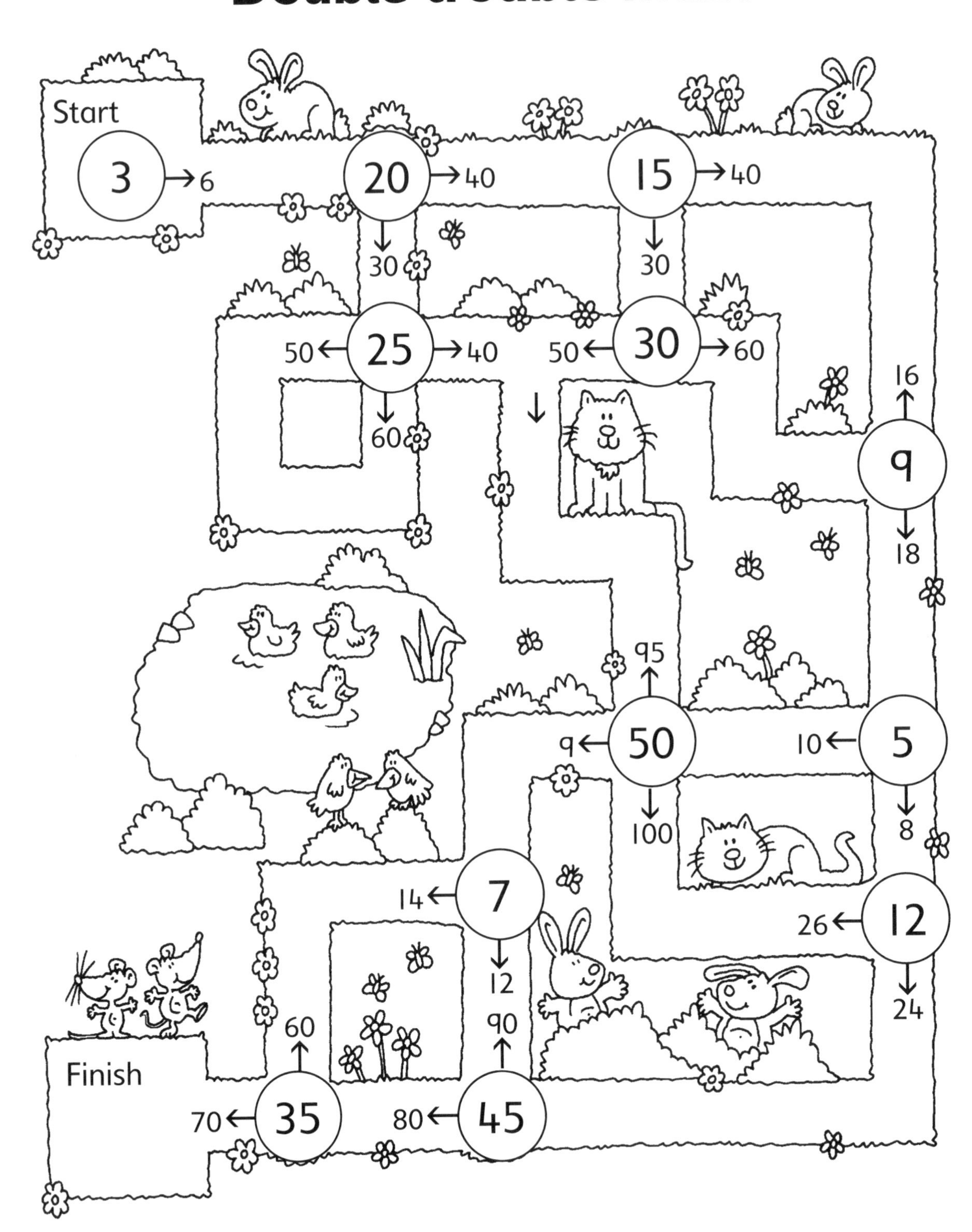


**Dear Helper**

This activity will help your child to practise doubling numbers. To travel through the maze, your child must correctly double each of the numbers in a circle and then follow the appropriate arrow. Ask your child to mark out their route and afterwards check they have gone the correct way. If your child has difficulty, ask them to add the number by splitting it into tens and units. For a challenge, ask them to make up their own 'Double trouble maze' using different numbers.

Name Date

# Which coins?

- Look at the coins above. Using the least amount of coins, make the total amount of money shown in the boxes below.

£1.25

£1 + 20p + 5 = £1.25

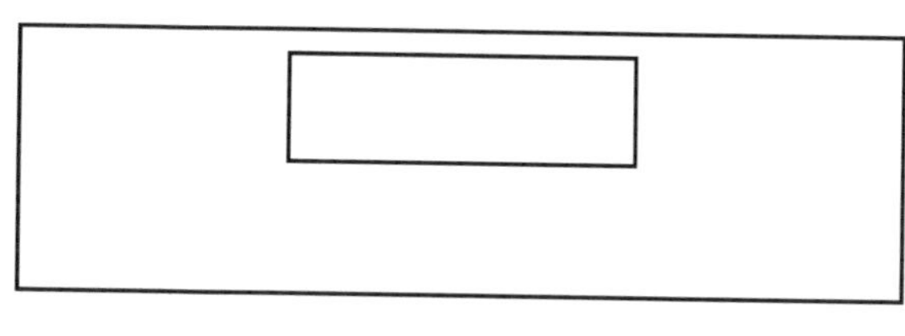

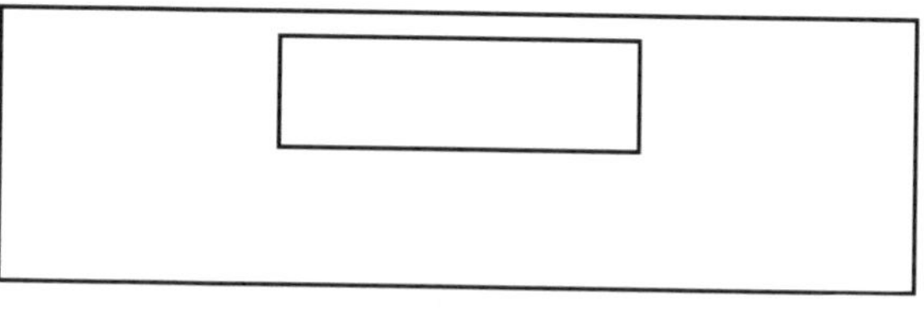

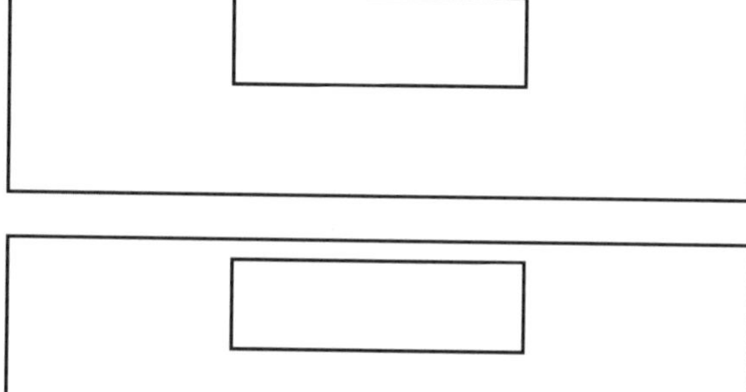

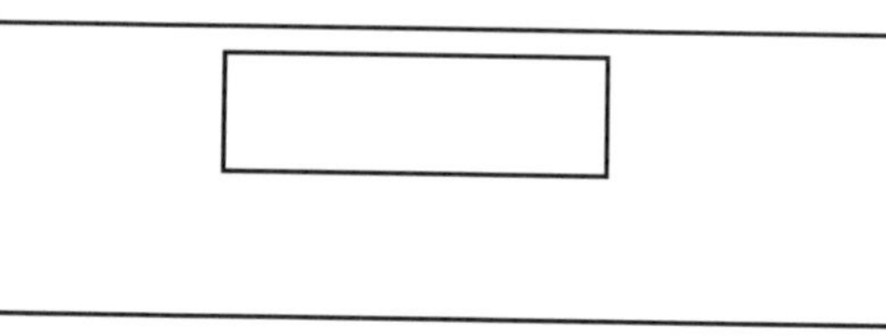

**Dear Helper**

Your child has been learning how to make different total amounts using different coins. Encourage them to use the least number of coins to make each total amount (they can use two or more of the same coin if necessary), and to write a number sentence to describe which coins they used. Your child's teacher has chosen appropriate amounts of money for your child to make. Please check that your child has correctly positioned the decimal point between pounds and pence. An example has been done for you.

ne Date

BLOCK B

# DJ Peejay

- DJ Peejay is trying to make his sound system work.
- Help him by connecting the wires on his equipment.
- Draw a line to connect each calculation to its answer.

**Dear Helper**
This activity helps your child to revise their 2-, 5- and 10-times tables. All children are expected to know the 2-, 5- and 10-times tables by the end of Key Stage 1 which is at the end of Year 2. If your child has any gaps in knowledge of these tables, then work hard at getting them to learn them. Learning tables off by heart gives children real confidence with maths and makes so many other areas of maths much easier.

Name Date

# The name game

- How many new two-digit numbers can you find in 15 minutes? Write each number, and its name in words, in the space below. For example, '47, forty seven'.

| 2 | 3 | 4 | 7 | 8 |
|---|---|---|---|---|

**Helpful words**

twenty two

thirty three

forty four

seventy seven

eighty eight

| 47, forty seven | |
|---|---|
| | |
| | |
| | |
| | |
| | |
| | |
| | |
| | |
| | |
| | |

**Dear Helper**

This activity will consolidate your child's knowledge of number names. Explain that you would like them to make two-digit numbers from the numbers at the top of the page. When they have made a new number, ask them to write it down in numerals and in words. After 15 minutes, ask them to stop and count how many numbers they have made. If they have difficulty, ask them to write single digits and words. If they want a challenge, ask them to make up and name three-digit numbers.

Name Date

# Get some help!

For example:

| 14 6 How many more? | My mum has 14 pairs of shoes. I have 6 pairs. How many more pairs has she got than me? | If I count from your 6 to your mum's 14, I get a difference of 8: 7, 8, 9, 10, 11, 12, 13, 14. |
|---|---|---|

| Facts | My word problem | My Helper's answer |
|---|---|---|
| 14 8 How many more? | | |
| 23 black dogs<br>12 white dogs |  | |
| 18 apples<br>8 pears |  | |
| 12 rabbits<br>15 guinea pigs | | 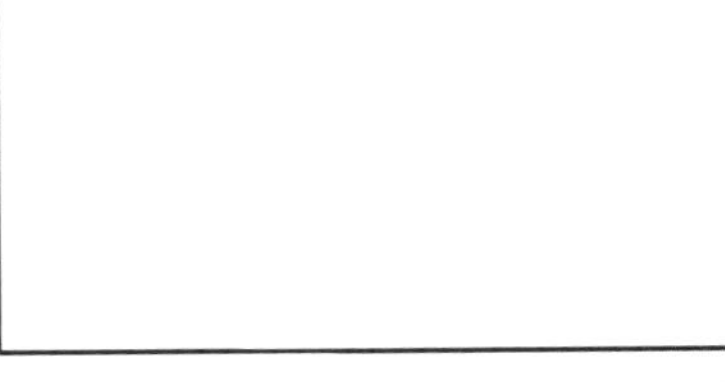 |
| 50 sweets<br>60 chews | |  |

**Dear Helper**

Invite your child to use the facts above as starting points for making up word problems for you to solve. Explain how you solved the problem and/or ask for your child's help. When you have solved each problem, ask your child if they can think of another way to work it out.

Name Date

# Beat the clock!

| | | |
|---|---|---|
| 6 + ☐ = 7 | 5 + ☐ = 7 | 2 + ☐ = 7 |
| 4 + ☐ = 7 | 2 + ☐ = 5 | 0 + ☐ = 5 |
| 3 + ☐ = 5 | 5 + ☐ = 5 | ☐ + 9 = 10 |
| ☐ + 3 = 10 | ☐ + 6 = 10 | ☐ + 2 = 10 |
| 9 – ☐ = 7 | 10 – ☐ = 7 | 10 – ☐ = 6 |
| 8 – ☐ = 7 | 7 – ☐ = 5 | 8 – ☐ = 5 |
| 9 – ☐ = 5 | 5 – ☐ = 5 | ☐ – 9 = 0 |
| ☐ – 3 = 5 | ☐ – 6 = 4 | ☐ – 2 = 7 |

**Dear Helper**

Your child has been learning by heart addition and subtraction facts for numbers to at least 10. Give your child ten minutes to complete as many sums as possible. If your child has difficulty, allow them to use counters to help them and do not time them. Reduce the time for children who would like a challenge.

Name Date

# Shape puzzle

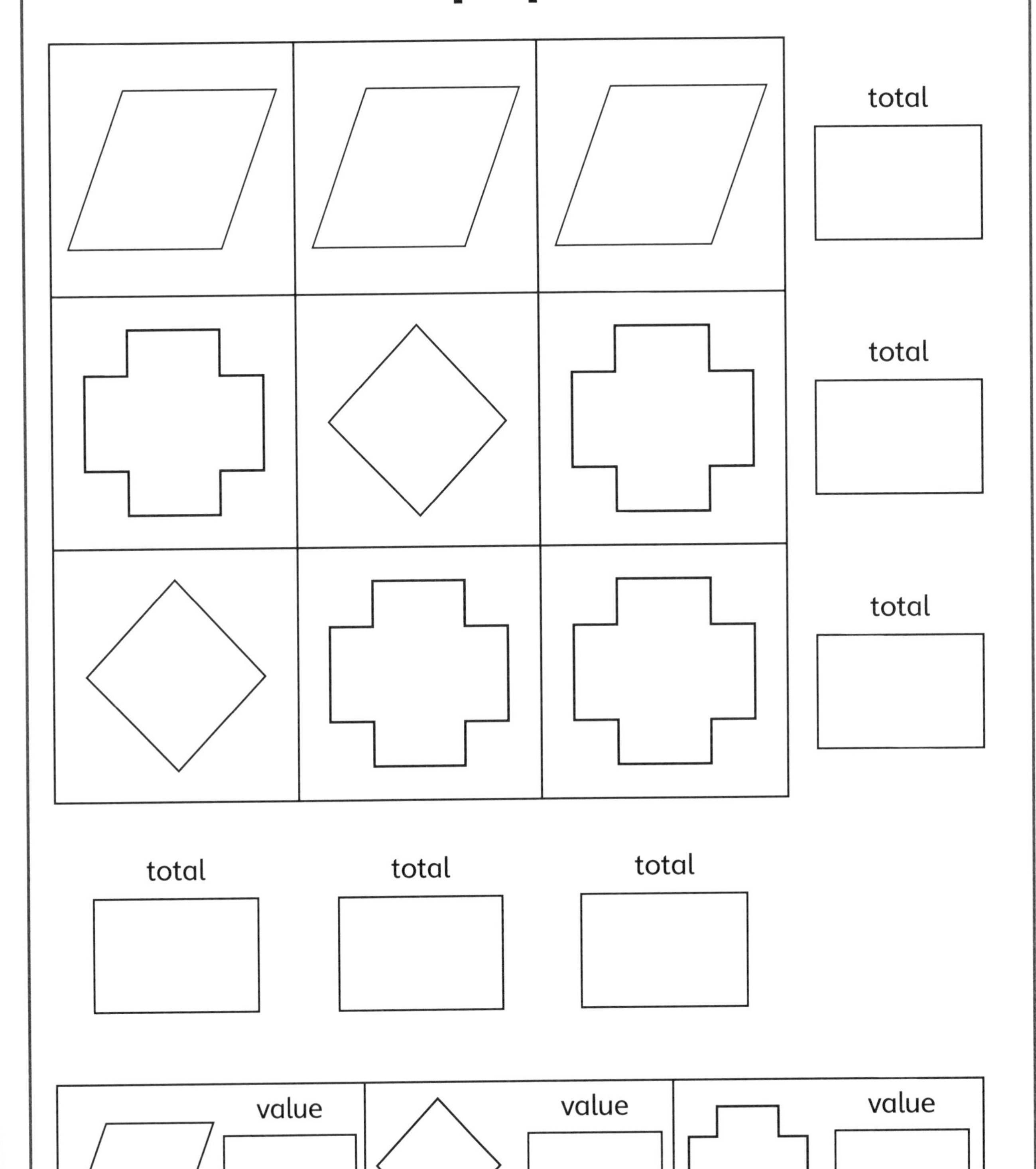


**Dear Helper**
Explain to your child that each shape above represents a different number. Your child's teacher will already have filled in some totals appropriate to your child's ability. Using these totals, help your child to work out the value of each shape, and then to work out the remaining totals.

Name Date

# Give us a clue!

- Match each statement to the correct shape below.

| I have four sides that are equal lengths. | I have three sides and three corners. |
|---|---|
| Shape: | Shape: |

| I have two faces shaped like circles. | I have one face shaped like a circle. |
|---|---|
| Shape: | Shape: |

| There is nothing straight about me at all. | I have at least two square faces. |
|---|---|
| Shape: | Shape: |

| I have a circular base and curved sides. | I have six faces. |
|---|---|
| Shape: | Shape: |

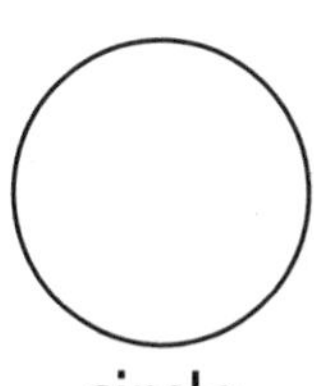
circle

square

triangle

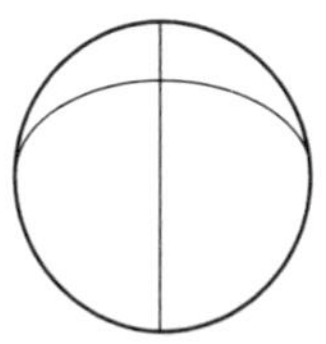
sphere

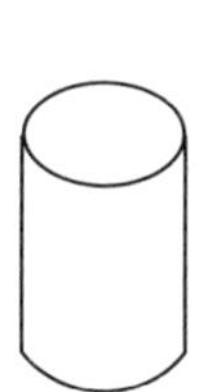
cylinder

cone

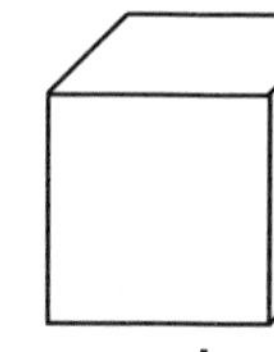
cube

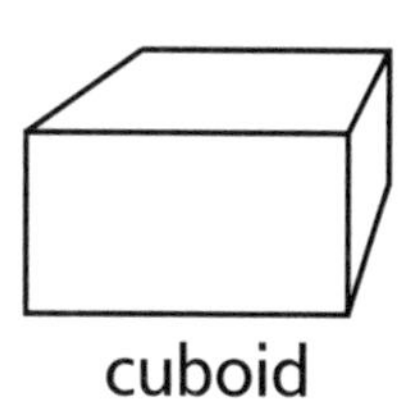
cuboid

**Dear Helper**

Your child has been learning about the properties of shapes. Read out the clues and ask your child to tell you the name of the shape and write the answer in the appropriate place. If your child has difficulty, ask them to point to the picture and write the name in for them. For a challenge, ask them to make up another clue for each shape.

Name Date

# Reflective symmetry

- Which of the letters in the words below have lines of symmetry?
  - Some have none, some have one, some have more than one.
  - The Y has one line of symmetry. It has been drawn for you.
- Use a ruler to draw dotted lines of symmetry on the rest of the letters.

LINES

OF

SYMMETRY

**Dear Helper**
This activity helps your child to practise finding lines of symmetry. Extend this activity by experimenting with your child to find the lines of symmetry in the rest of the letters of the alphabet. Draw them in block lettering on the back of this sheet. You could also look through newspapers or magazines to find symmetrical pictures, logos and patterns. Draw the lines of symmetry with a felt-tipped pen.

Name Date

# Rounding up

My numbers are: My estimate is: My answer is:

How I worked out the answer:

My numbers are: My estimate is: My answer is:

How I worked out the answer:

My numbers are: My estimate is: My answer is:

How I worked out the answer:

**Dear Helper**

Your child has been learning how to estimate an answer to a calculation before working it out, by using a rounding strategy. Ask your child to choose three different numbers from the boxes at the top of the page. (The numbers in the boxes have been chosen to match your child's abilities.) Challenge your child to estimate what the answer will be when the three numbers are added together, and to write the estimate in the box, before working out the correct answer. Encourage them to write down the strategy they used. Repeat the activity using different numbers.

ame Date

# Making problems

- Use the number facts on this sheet to make up problems for your Helper to answer.

£5

£4.50

My problem:

The answer:

£1.50

2

My problem:

The answer:

£1.50

£5

My problem:

The answer:

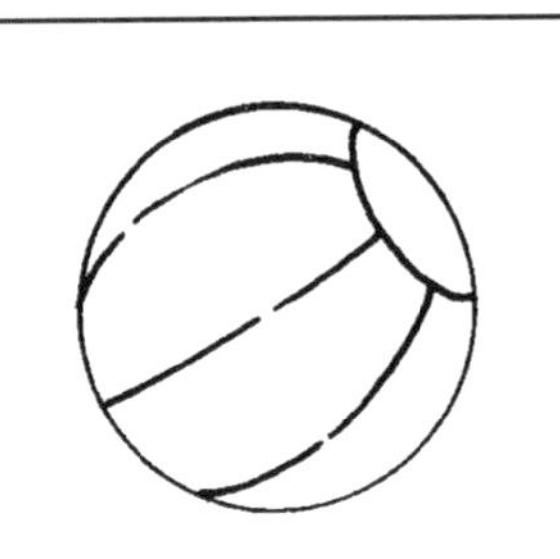

75p

10

My problem:

The answer:

**Dear Helper**

Encourage your child to use the facts on this sheet to make up some problems for you to answer. For example: *I would like to buy two books, each costing £1.50. How much money will I need?* Extend the problem by asking: *How much change will I get if I pay with £5?* If your child has difficulty, write the problems for them and let them use real coins and notes. For a challenge, encourage them to make up some more problems with their own amounts of money.

Name Date

# Right or wrong?

■ Read the statements below and decide whether they are right or wrong.

**Statement 1**

This is a cylinder.

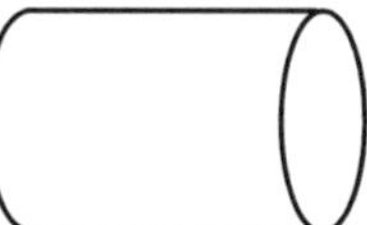

This is right/wrong because

**Statement 2**

21 is an odd number.

This is right/wrong because

**Statement 3**

I can make 10p using 1p, 2p, 5p and 10p coins in just three different ways.

This is right/wrong because

**Dear Helper**

Your child has been investigating statements and proving that they are right or wrong. Encourage your child to work through the given statements, explaining why they think each one is right or wrong. If your child's explanation is quite lengthy, and they are having difficulty, please help them to write it down.

Name Date

# What a problem!

■ Solve the problems below. Show how you worked them out.

| | |
|---|---|
| Four oranges cost ☐ each.<br>How much change would you get from ☐ ?<br>Show your working out. | Three apples cost ☐ each.<br>How much change would you get from ☐ ?<br>Show your working out. |
| Five pears cost ☐ each.<br>How much change would you get from ☐ ?<br>Show your working out. | Three apples cost ☐ each.<br>How much change would you get from ☐ ?<br>Show your working out. |
| Ten bananas cost ☐ each.<br>How much change would you get from ☐ ?<br>Show your working out. | Two biscuits cost ☐ each.<br>How much change would you get from ☐ ?<br>Show your working out. |

■ Make up some problems on the back of the sheet for your Helper to answer.

**Dear Helper**
This activity will provide your child with practice in solving word problems. Your child's teacher will have chosen numbers in each example to match your child's ability.

Name Date

# Doubles and halves

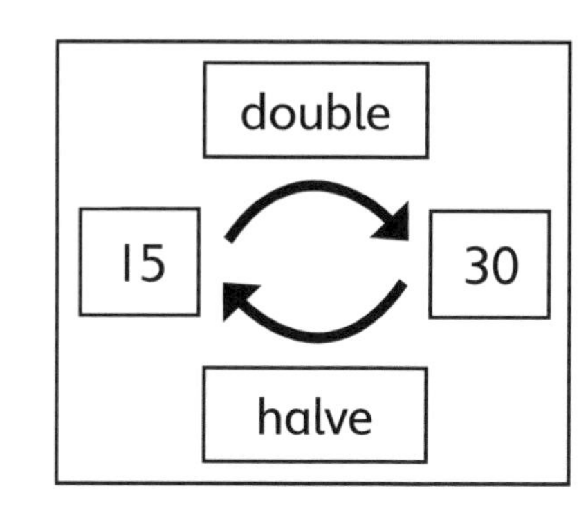

- Double or halve the numbers below to fill in the missing boxes.

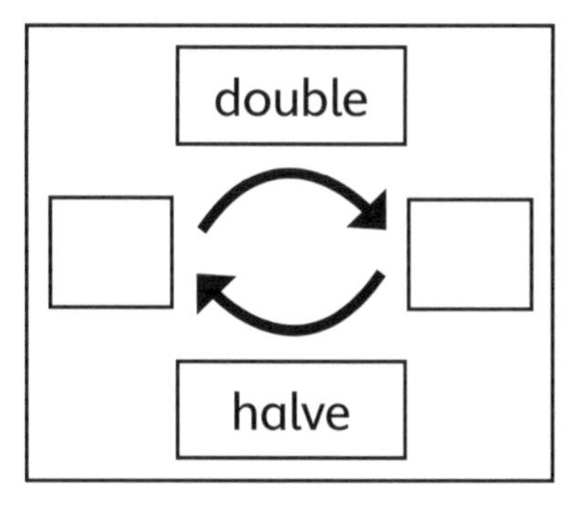


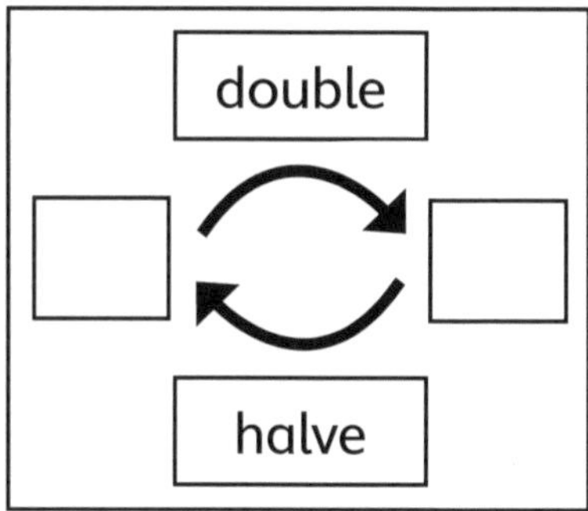


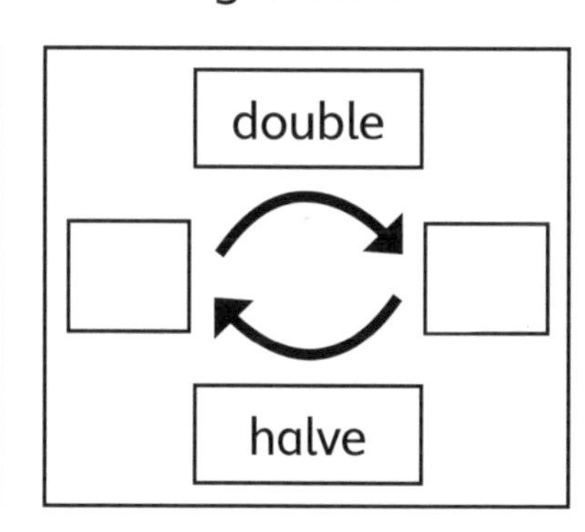


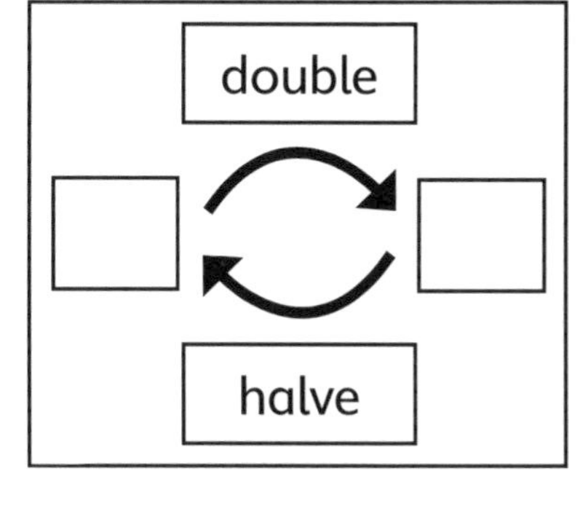


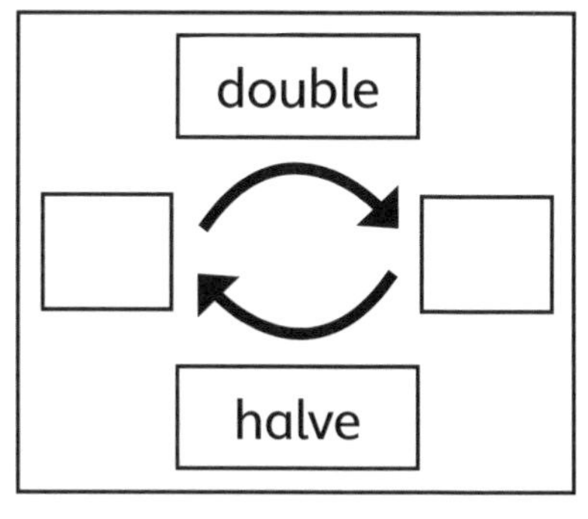


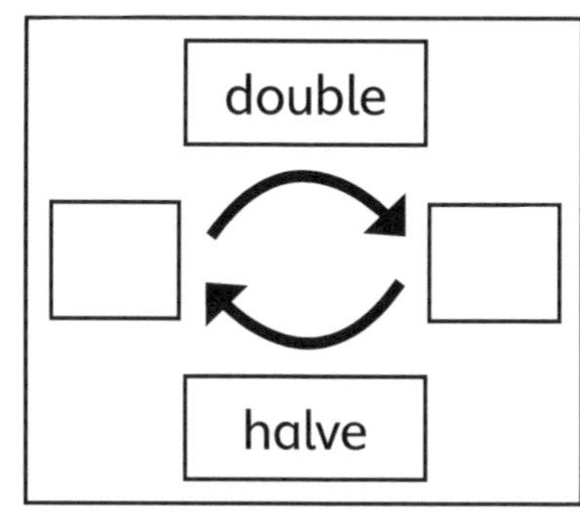


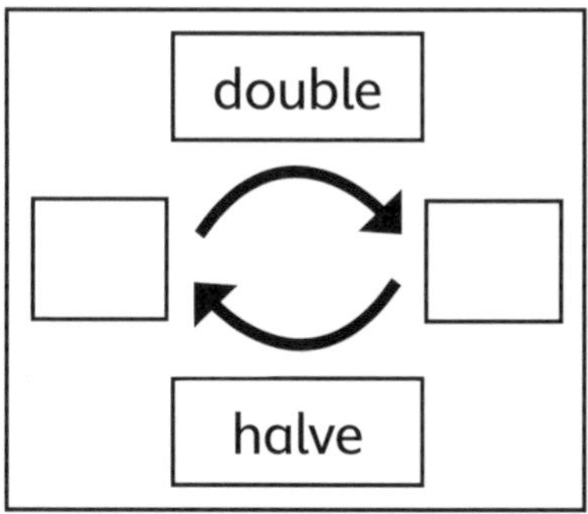


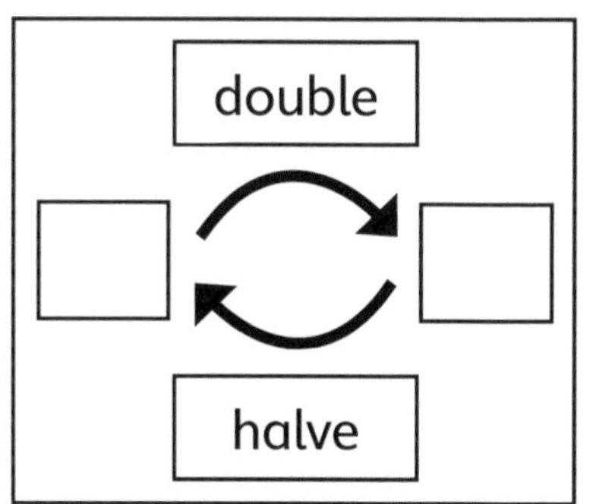


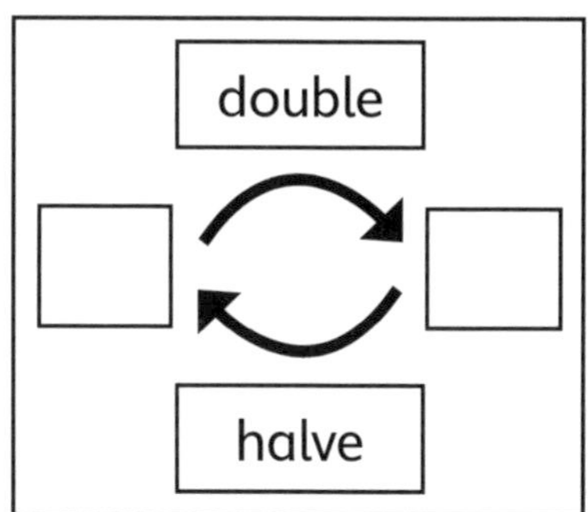


**Dear Helper**

This activity will provide practice in doubling and halving numbers. Remind your child that doubling is making something twice as big, and halving is making it half as big. Your child's teacher will have chosen numbers appropriate to your child's ability. An example has been done for you.

Name Date

# You are the teacher!

- You are the teacher today!
- Mark these two tests.
- Put a tick next to the correct answers.
- Write the total scores at the bottom of each child's work.

| Jimmy | Grace |
| --- | --- |
| 1) 6 + 7 = 14 | 1) 8 – 5 = 4 |
| 2) 8 + 5 = 12 | 2) 13 – 6 = 7 |
| 3) 12 + 6 = 18 | 3) 11 – 8 = 3 |
| 4) 9 + 4 = 13 | 4) 17 – 9 = 6 |
| 5) 15 + 8 = 22 | 5) 24 – 10 = 14 |
| Total: /5 | Total: /5 |

**Dear Helper**
This activity helps your child to learn to check their own work. It is always worth checking your answers to calculations so it is a habit that your child should get into very quickly. As an additional challenge, ask your child to write down all the correct answers on the back of this sheet.

| Activity | Learning objectives | Managing the homework |
| --- | --- | --- |
| **C1** | | |
| **Measures**<br>Read scales to measure length, mass and capacity. | Read the numbered divisions on a scale, and interpret the divisions between them (for example, on a scale from 0 to 25 with intervals of 1 shown but only the divisions 0, 5, 10, 15 and 20 numbered); use a ruler to measure lines to the nearest centimetre | **Before:** Tell the children that their homework is to practise reading scales either exactly or to the nearest measurement.<br>**After:** Photocopy a homework sheet onto an OHT and work through it with the children. |
| **Reading scales**<br>Draw and measure length, mass and capacity. | Read the numbered divisions on a scale, and interpret the divisions between them (for example, on a scale from 0 to 25 with intervals of 1 shown but only the divisions 0, 5, 10, 15 and 20 numbered); use a ruler to measure lines to the nearest centimetre | **Before:** Tell the children that their homework is to practise reading scales either exactly or to the nearest measurement. Make sure everyone has access to a ruler, kitchen scales and a measuring jug at home.<br>**After:** Photocopy the homework sheet onto an OHT and work through it with the children. |
| **Sorting it out**<br>Solve a problem using data from a list and make up a block graph. | Answer a question by collecting and recording data in lists and tables; represent the data in lists and tables; represent the data as block graphs to show results | **Before:** Remind the children about block graphs and pictograms. Show them the homework on an OHT and ask what labels need to be written on the axes of the graph. Discuss how you can show how many children like each paint colour.<br>**After:** Look at the children's results and ask questions such as: *How many children were in the class? Which was the most popular colour?* |
| **How long is it?**<br>Measure household objects with a ruler. | Estimate, compare and measure lengths, weights and capacities, choosing and using standard units (m, cm, kg, litre) and suitable measuring instruments | **Before:** Make sure everyone has access to a ruler at home.<br>**After:** Estimate and measure the height of class members who weren't measured at home. |
| **C2** | | |
| **Favourite colours**<br>List the facts that you can find from a pictogram. | Answer a question by collecting and recording data in lists and tables; represent the data in lists and tables; represent the data as pictograms to show results | **Before:** Tell the children that they are going to list as many facts as they can from the pictogram on the homework sheet. Explain that they can use numbers instead of words - for example, '5 like red'.<br>**After:** Invite the children to share some of the facts that they found. |
| **Faulty graph**<br>Identify and correct seven mistakes in a block graph. | Answer a question by collecting and recording data in lists and tables; represent the data in lists and tables; represent the data as block graphs to show results | **Before:** Show the children an OHT of the faulty graph with seven mistakes for them to find; ask for examples. Explain that they should find as many mistakes as they can, and correct them.<br>**After:** Show the OHT again and ask for volunteers to correct a mistake, explaining why it is wrong. Assess their adeptness at doing this. Invite other children to share information that they wrote down from the corrected graph. |
| **Sort it out!**<br>Find the 'odd one out' from tables of information. | Use lists, tables and diagrams to sort objects; explain choices using appropriate language, including 'not' | **Before:** Encourage the children to work through the problems in a systematic way.<br>**After:** Go through the homework with the class and compare methods and answers. |
| **Slippery Sid**<br>Use a ruler to measure objects to the nearest centimetre. | Read the numbered divisions on a scale; use a ruler to draw and measure lines to the nearest centimetre | **Before:** Make sure everyone has access to a ruler at home.<br>**After:** Compare the children's drawings of Slippery Sue, the 12cm snake. Are they all the same length? |

BLOCK C

## Handling data and measures

| Activity | Learning objectives | Managing the homework |
|---|---|---|
| **C3** | | |
| **Measure it**<br>Read centimetre, kilogram and litre scales. | Read the numbered divisions on a scale, and interpret the divisions between them (for example, on a scale from 0 to 25 with intervals of 1 shown but only the divisions 0, 5, 10, 15 and 20 numbered); use a ruler to measure lines to the nearest centimetre | **Before:** Tell the children that their homework is to practise reading scales either exactly or to the nearest measurement. Work through examples of reading scales using the OHP.<br>**After:** Using an OHT copy of the homework sheet, invite children to show how they read the scales and to give their answers. |
| **Draw the measures**<br>Indicate length, mass and volume on different types of measuring equipment. | Read the numbered divisions on a scale, and interpret the divisions between them (for example, on a scale from 0 to 25 with intervals of 1 shown but only the divisions 0, 5, 10, 15 and 20 numbered) | **Before:** Work through some examples using a copy of the homework sheet on the overhead projector.<br>**After:** Using an OHT copy of the homework sheet, invite children to draw arrows to indicate the amounts required on the measuring equipment. Ask how they knew where to draw their arrow. |
| **Animal information**<br>Fill in a table of information and answer questions about it. | Follow a line of enquiry; answer questions by choosing and using suitable equipment and selecting, organising and presenting information in lists, tables and simple diagrams | **Before:** Show the children a completed example of the type of table in the activity.<br>**After:** Go through the answers with the class. You could conduct the same survey within the class and have the children tabulate the results. |
| **Tasty take-aways**<br>Complete a pictogram based on a given set of data. | Use lists, tables and diagrams to sort objects; explain choices using appropriate language, including 'not' | **Before:** Show the class an example of a completed pictogram.<br>**After:** Ask the children questions about the data they have displayed in their pictograms. |

Name Date

# Measures

■ Record the correct measurements on the lines below.

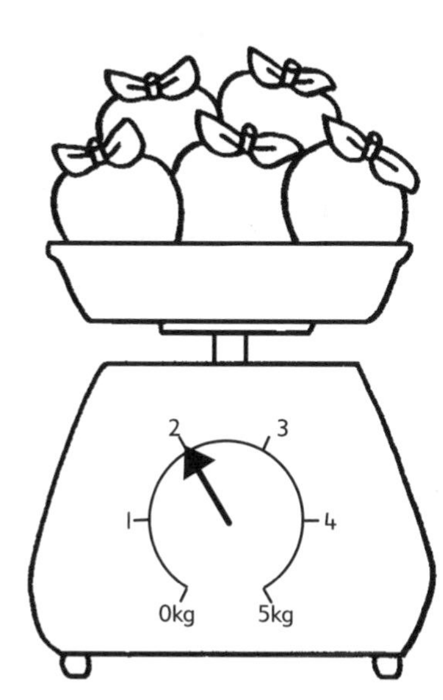


The apples weigh

______ kg.

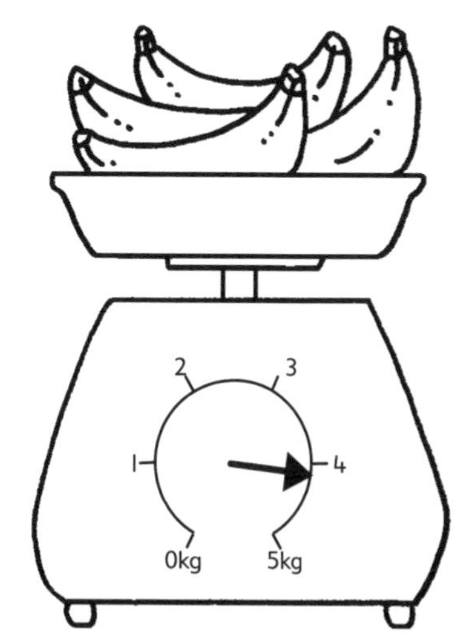


The bananas weigh just

over ______ kg.

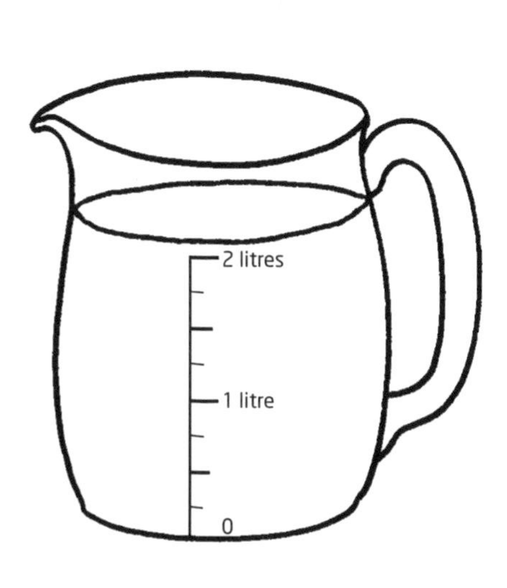


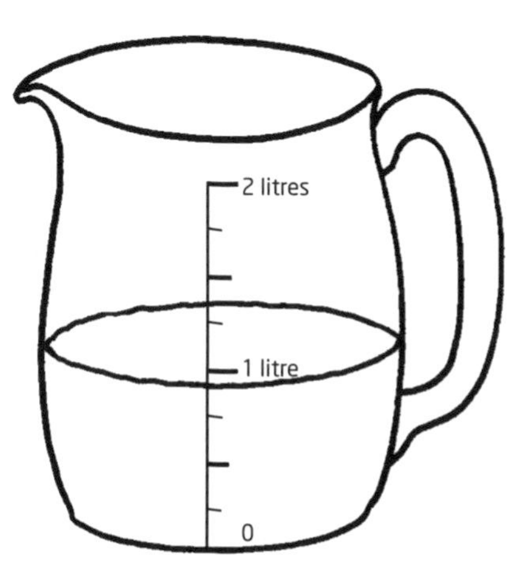


The string is

______ cm long.

There is just over ______

litres of liquid in the jug.

There is just under ______

litres of liquid in the jug.

**Dear Helper**

Please help your child to read the scales to work out the answers. Encourage your child to write the answers in the spaces provided. If your child has difficulty, count along each scale with them in the appropriate intervals. For a challenge, encourage them to try to give an accurate reading.

Name Date

# Reading scales

- Measure this line and record your answer in the box.

The length of this line is:



- Measure flour or sugar on to some scales so that they show the same weight as the scales on this sheet.

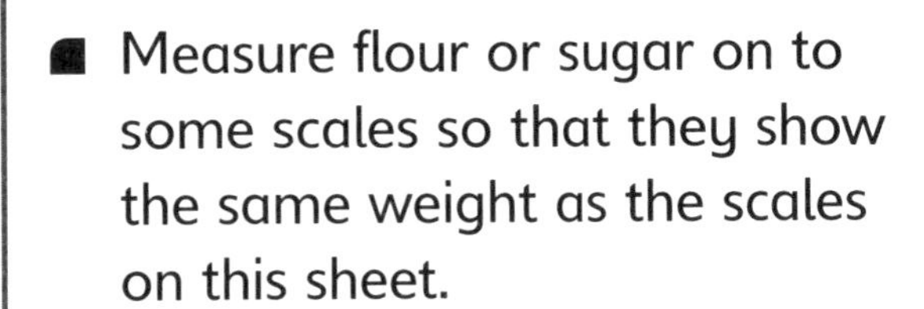

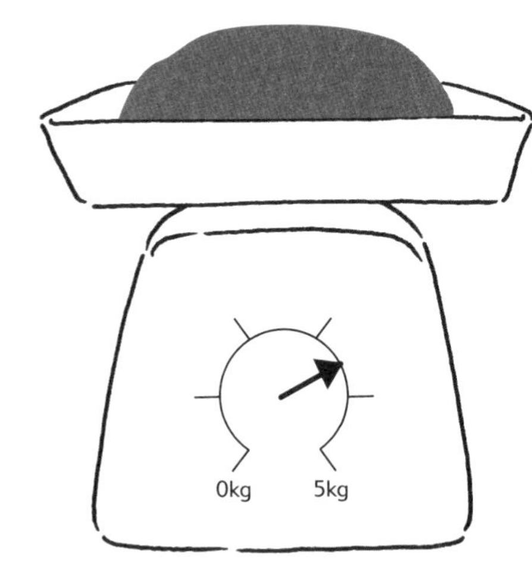


This weight is:

- Can you measure water into a measuring jug so that it looks the same as the jug on this sheet?

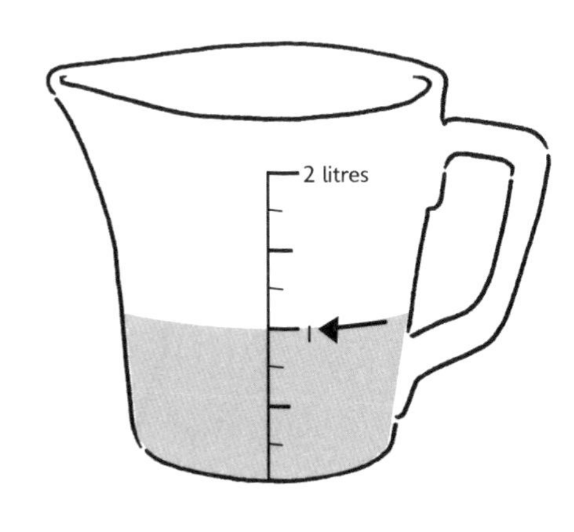


This volume is:

**Dear Helper**

This activity will reinforce the work that your child has been doing on reading measures. Work through the questions together, letting your child practically measure out the amounts for volume and weight if possible, and encourage them to write their answers in the boxes. Please provide a ruler for your child, as well as suitable scales and a measuring jug. If your child has difficulty, guide them with your finger for the ruler work and mark on the intervals on the scales and jug.

 

Name Date

# Sorting it out

**Problem**

I would like to order some paint for art, but I need you to help me decide which three colours to buy. I asked the class to tell me their favourite colours, and this is what they said:

| | | |
|---|---|---|
| 2 liked black | 3 liked orange | 4 liked red |
| 1 liked green | 10 liked yellow | 6 liked white |

- Which are the three most popular colours? Add the information to the block graph to show the results.

Number of children

Colours

**Dear Helper**

This activity will reinforce the work that your child has been doing on organising data. Read the problem above together, then look at the data in the box. Encourage your child to fill in numbers (1–10) on the vertical axis, and the colours on the horizontal axis, then help them to complete the block graph to show the information and answer the problem. If your child has difficulty, help them to label the axis. For a challenge, ask them to make up a block graph to solve their own problem.

Name Date

# How long is it?

- You will need:
  - a ruler
  - a number of household objects.

| Object | Estimate (cm) | Actual length (cm) |
|---|---|---|
| CD | | |
| DVD | | |
| Telephone | | |
| Newspaper | | |
| Teaspoon | | |
| Floor rug | | |
| Favourite toy | | |

- Find the objects listed around the house.
- Estimate their lengths in centimetres (cm) and write your estimate in the table. (Remember, an estimate is a good guess.)
- Measure the objects with your ruler and write the actual lengths in the table.
- How close were your estimates to the final measurement?

**Dear Helper**
This activity helps your child to practise measuring objects. Here is another fun measuring activity: children are fascinated by how tall they are. You could help them measure the height of all the members of the family and present the data as a poster. Who do they think will get taller? Who will stay the same height? Will anyone get shorter? Repeat the exercise in six months' time to find out!

Name Date

# Favourite colours

- Write as many sentences as you can based on the data below. If you need more space, use the back of this sheet.
- Each smiley face stands for one child.

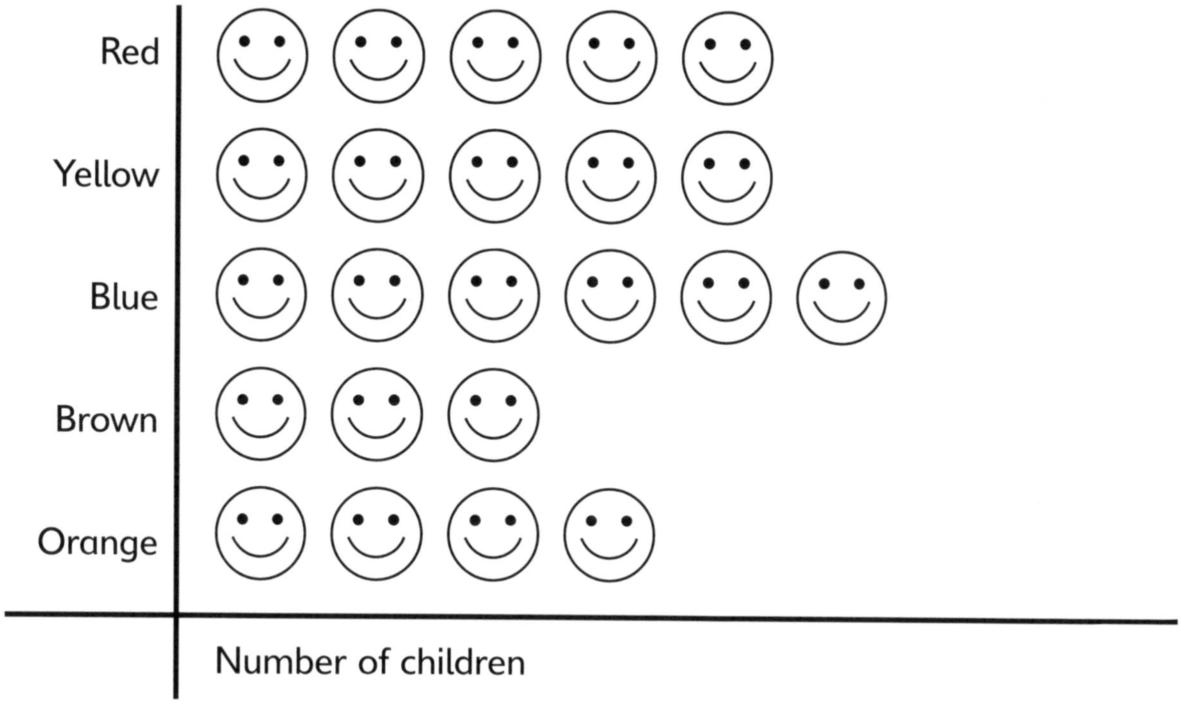

Red

Yellow

Blue

Brown

Orange

Number of children

1. One more child likes orange than likes brown.
2. Blue is the most popular colour.

**Dear Helper**

This activity will consolidate the work on data handling that your child has been doing at school. Ask your child to look at the pictogram above. Each smiley face represents one child. Encourage your child to use the space beneath the pictogram to write down as many things as possible about what the data is telling them. Two examples have been given.

Name Date

# Faulty graph

- Find seven faults with the graph shown below. Correct the graph and then write down as many facts as you can using the information provided.

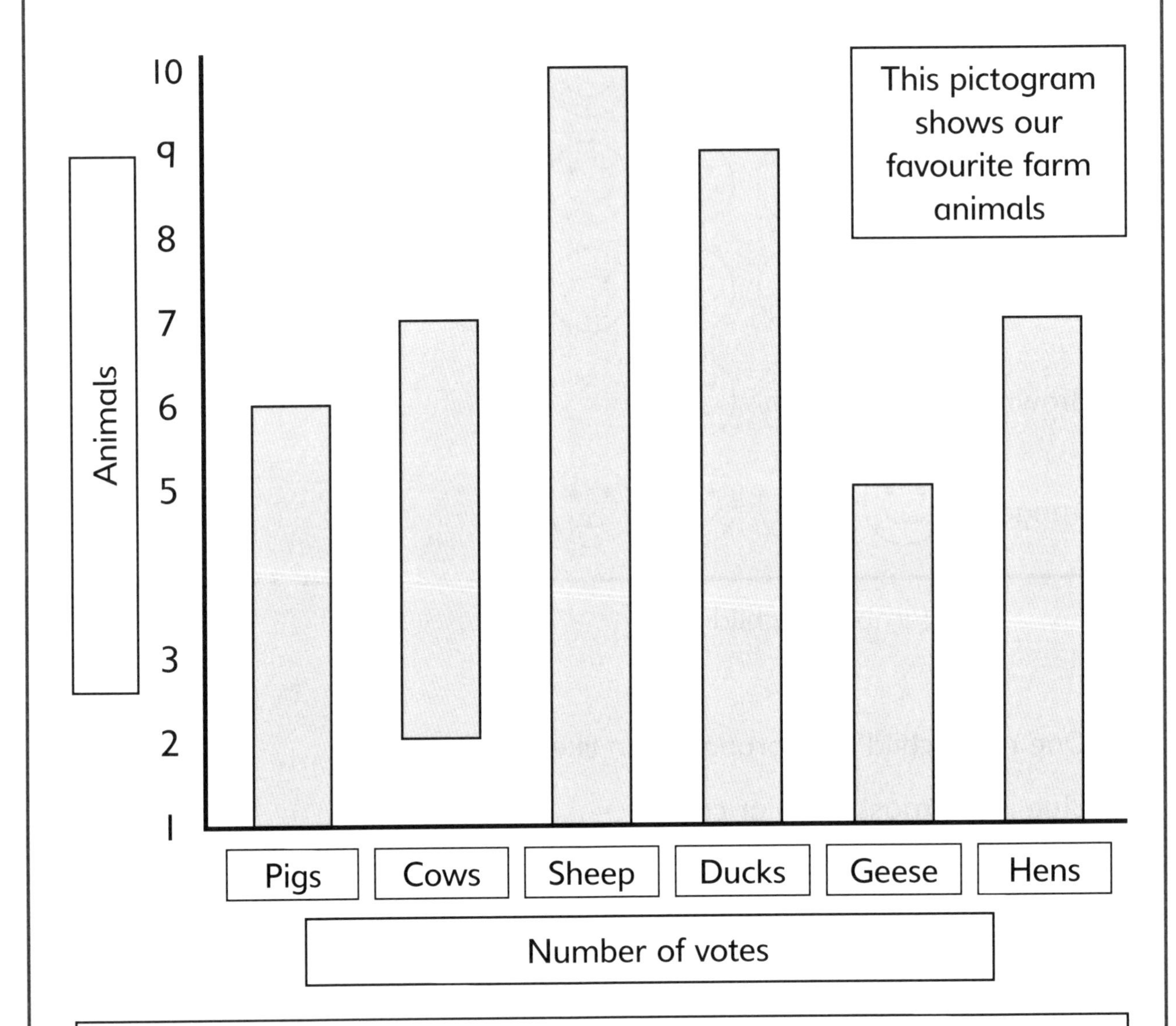


The votes for our favourite farm animals were:

Pigs 6 Cows 5 Sheep 10 Ducks 9 Geese 5 Hens 5

**Dear Helper**

This activity will provide practice in organising data. There are lots of mistakes on this graph for your child to find and correct. Help your child to find them all and to draw or write on the correct answers. When they have found the faults, encourage them to write down as many facts as they can find from the graph (for example, the favourite and least favourite animals). If your child has difficulty, ask them to point at things that look wrong in the graph. For a challenge, ask them to draw a correct graph.

Name Date

# Sort it out!

- Hoarding Harry has boxes of items all over his house!
- Some of the things he has collected are in the wrong boxes.
- Circle the ones you think are in the wrong boxes.

**Dear Helper**
This activity helps your child get to grips with information they have in front of them. Encourage your child to work systematically and methodically and to think carefully about what they are asked to do.

Name Date

# Slippery Sid

- You need a ruler for this activity.

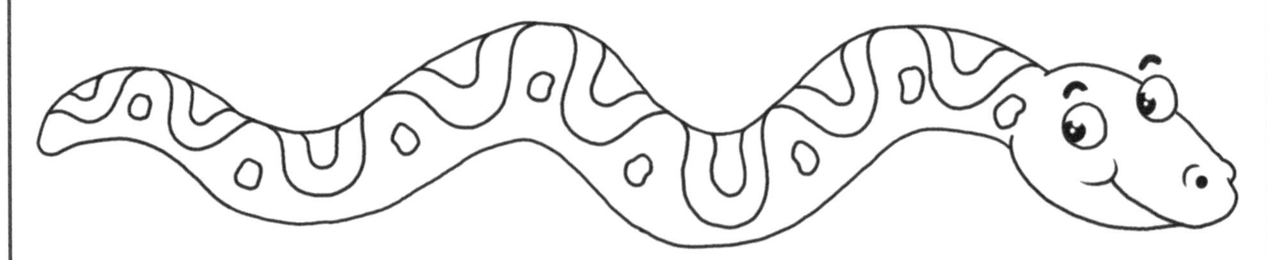

- Slippery Sid is having his friends over to stay and is making them new beds to sleep in. He needs to know how long they are!
- Measure Sid's friends to the nearest centimetre.

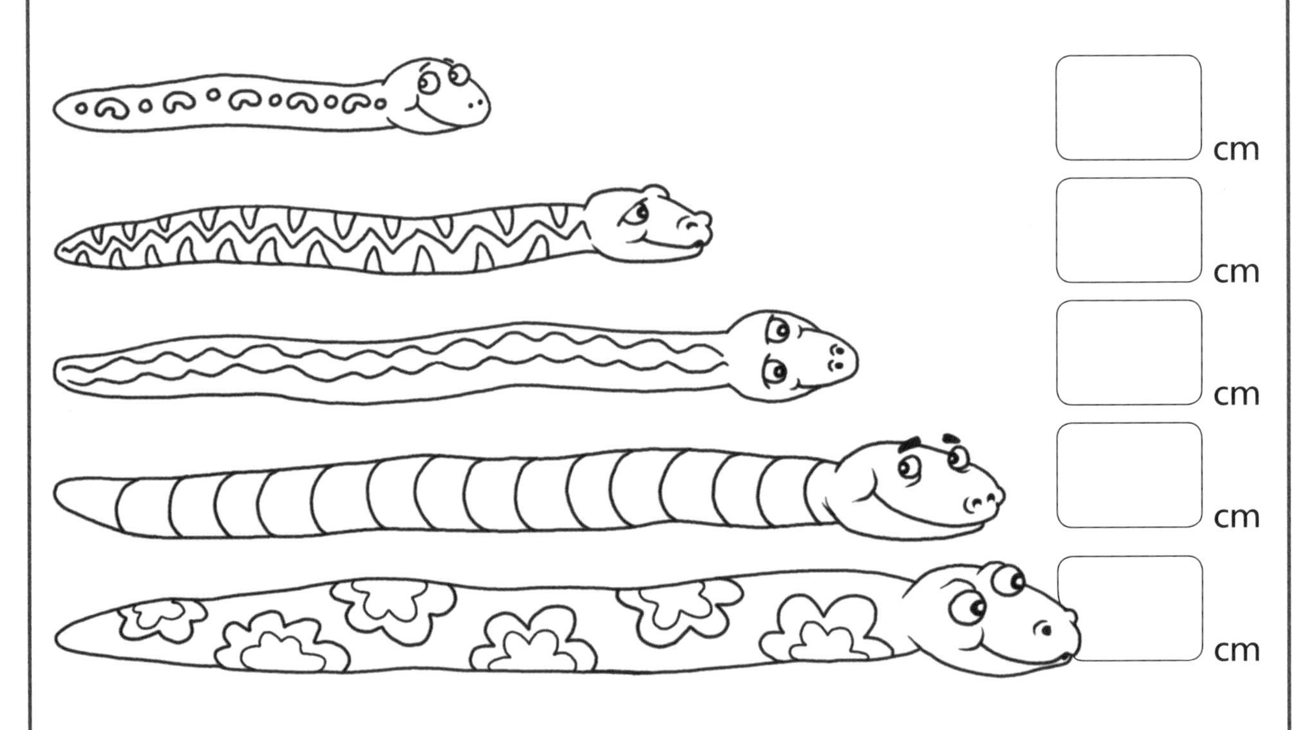


- Sid's sister, Slippery Sue, is 12cm long. Draw a picture of Sue here.

**Dear Helper**
This activity helps your child to measure and draw accurately using a ruler. Helpful hints include holding it steady so it doesn't slip and reading the scale from 0cm rather than from 1cm, which is a common mistake.

Name Date

# Measure it

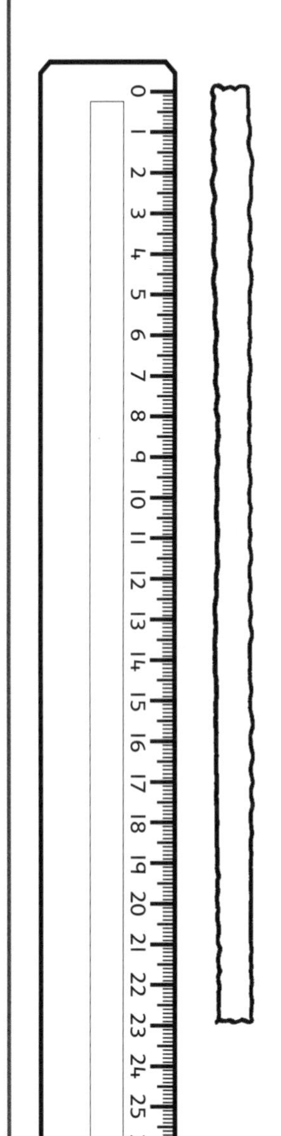


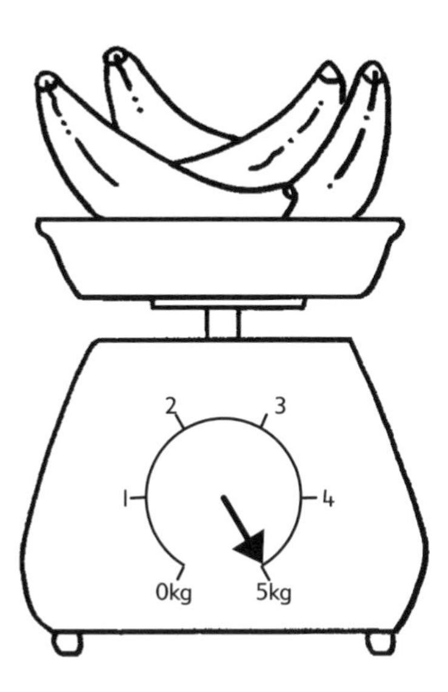


The bananas weigh ______ kg.

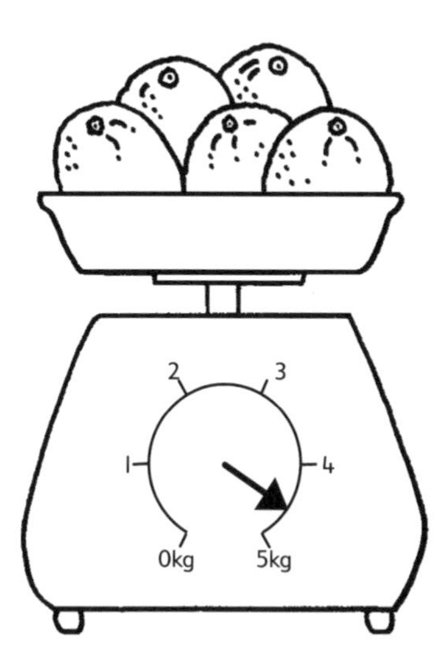


The oranges weigh just over ______ kg.

The ribbon is ______ cm long.

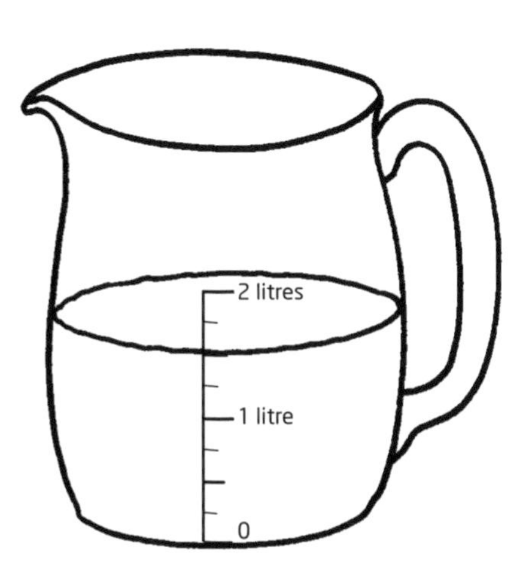


There are ______ litres of liquid in the jug.

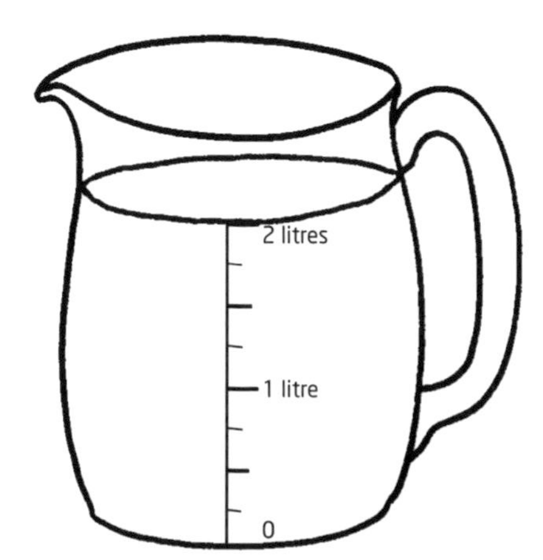


There are ______ litres of liquid in the jug.

**Dear Helper**

This activity will reinforce the work on measures that your child has been doing in class. Encourage your child to read the measurements for each picture and to write the answers in the boxes.

Name Date

# Draw the measures

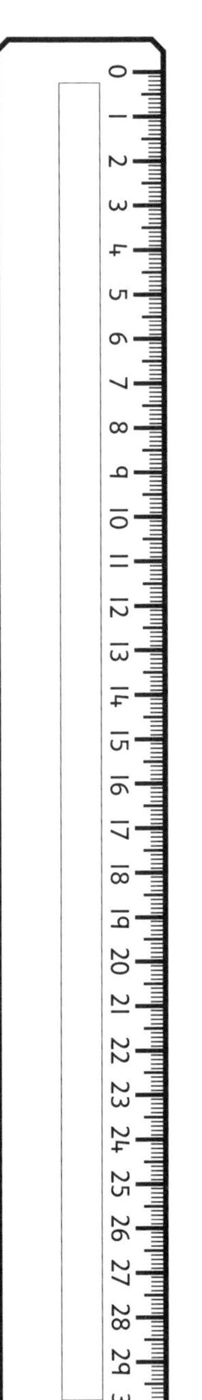

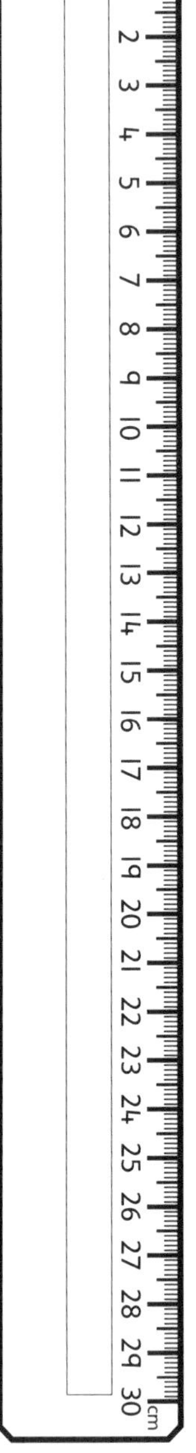

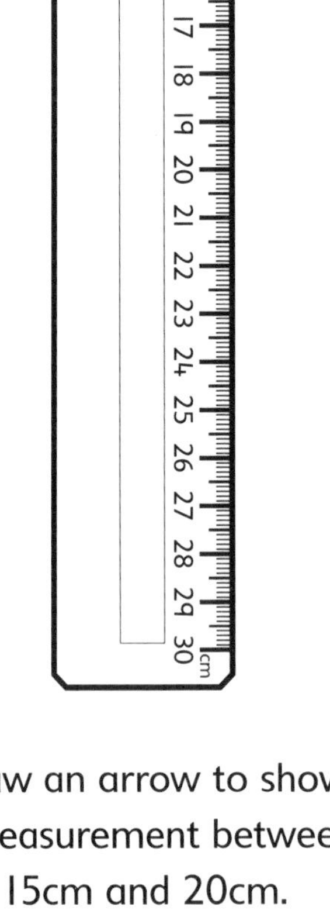

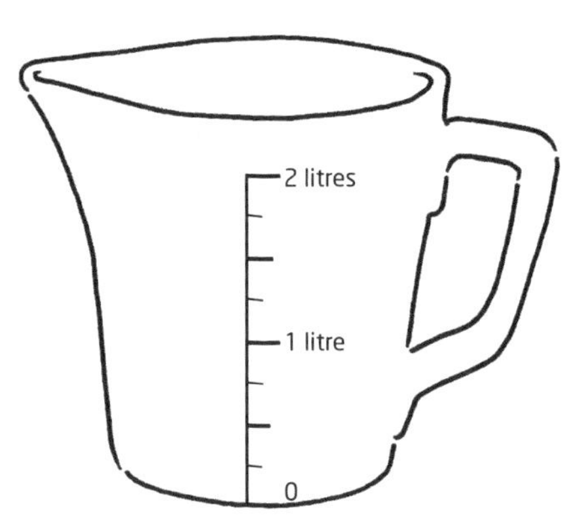


Draw an arrow to show half a litre.

Draw an arrow to show quarter of a litre.

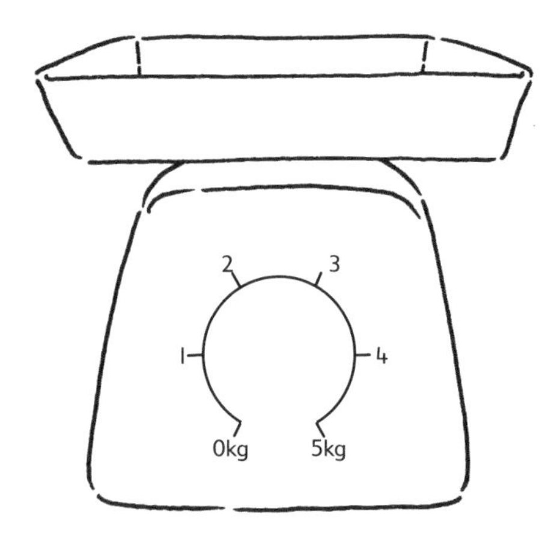


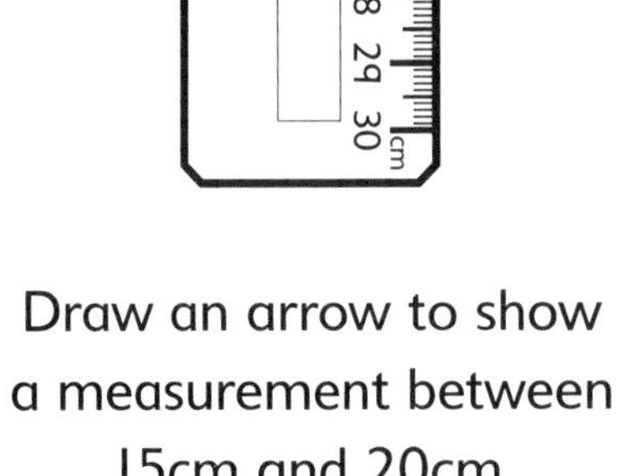

Draw an arrow to show 15cm.

Draw an arrow to show a measurement between 15cm and 20cm.

Draw an arrow to show 4.5kg.

**Dear Helper**
This activity will help to reinforce the work that your child has been doing on measures. Encourage your child to look at each picture in turn and read the instructions, then help them to draw an arrow on each picture in the appropriate place.

Name Date

# Animal information

- Oak Class did a survey about favourite wild animals.
- This is what they found out:

  7 children liked lions

  8 children liked tigers

  2 children liked crocodiles

  5 children liked gorillas

  3 children liked bears

  1 child liked spiders

- Add the information to the table, then answer the questions below.

## Favourite wild animals

| | Lions | Tigers | Crocodiles | Gorillas | Bears | Spiders |
|---|---|---|---|---|---|---|
| Number of children | | | | | | |

**1.** Which was the most popular wild animal? ____________

**2.** Which was the least popular? ____________

**3.** How many children were asked altogether? ____________

**Dear Helper**
This activity helps your child to organise, present and interpret data in a table. Encourage your child to look carefully at the information and make sure they understand what they are being asked to do. Explain to your child that presenting information, or data, in a table, chart or graph can make it easier to read.

Name Date

# Tasty take-aways

- Josh did a survey to find out which was the most popular take-away food. Here are his results:

  5 children liked pizza

  3 children liked burgers

  9 children like fish and chips

  4 children liked Chinese

  6 children liked curry

  2 children liked hotdogs

- Use this information to complete the pictogram below.

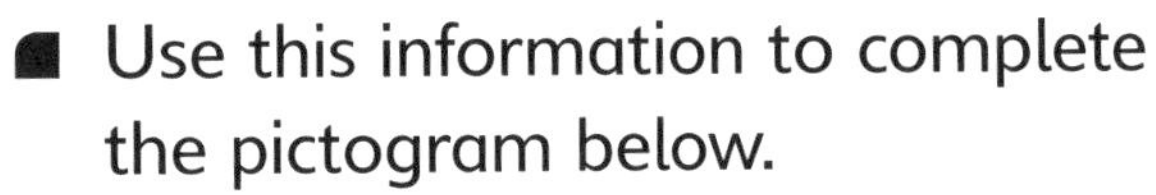

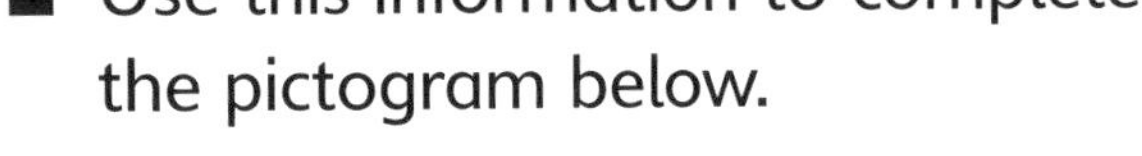

- Use ☺ as your symbol for each child.

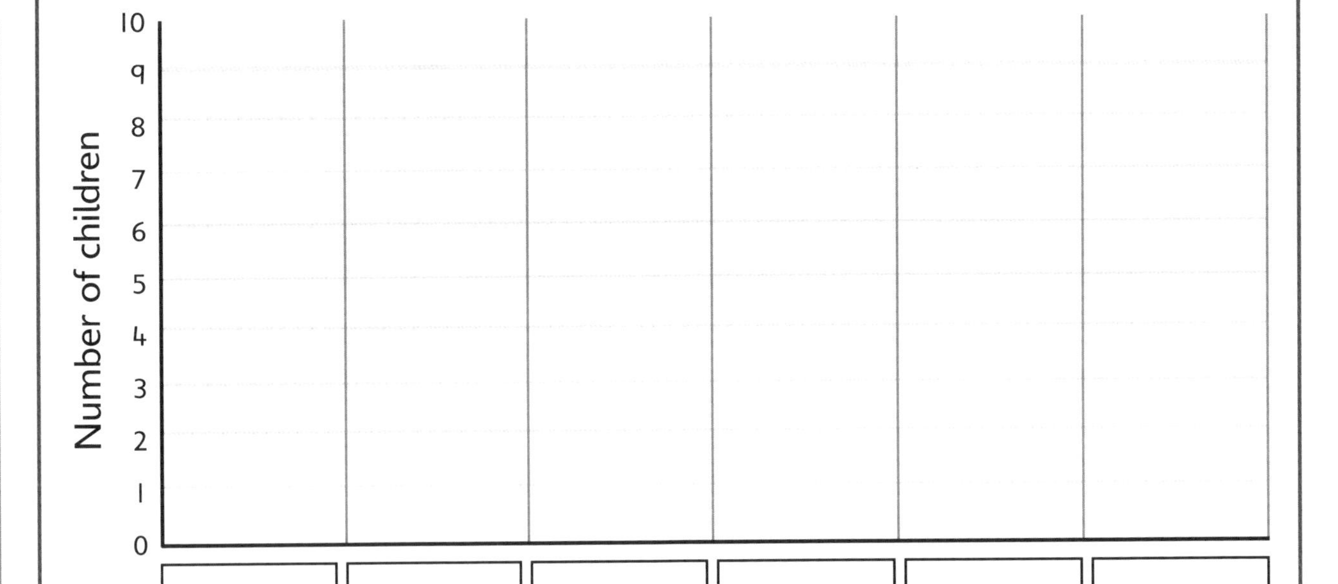


**Dear Helper**
This activity helps your child to become more confident at creating pictograms. Pictograms are a clear way for children to present their data and a good introduction to using and creating more complex graphs. Encourage your child to read questions more than once so they have a clear idea of what they have been asked to do.

# Calculating, measuring and understanding shape

| Activity | Learning objectives | Managing the homework |
|---|---|---|
| **D1** | | |
| **Time for snap!**<br>Play a card-matching game. | Use units of time (seconds, minutes, hours, days) and know the relationships between them | **Before:** Explain to the children that this is a Snap game to help them revise the relationship between units of time (for example, that 60 seconds is the same as one minute). Play the game as a class, working in two teams.<br>**After:** Recap how many seconds there are in a minute, minutes in an hour, hours in a day and so on. Observe how quickly the children can recall these facts. |
| **Which method?**<br>Choose the best strategy to use to solve a calculation. | • Solve problems involving addition, subtraction, multiplication or division in contexts of numbers, measures or pounds and pence<br>• Add or subtract mentally a single-digit number or a multiple of 10 to or from any two-digit number; use practical and informal written methods to add and subtract two-digit numbers | **Before:** Make differentiated versions of the worksheet by filling in the calculations according to the children's ability. Discuss possible strategies: near doubles, counting on, partitioning, rounding and number bonds. Demonstrate how to complete the activity.<br>**After:** Discuss each strategy and ask the children to suggest an appropriate calculation to use each one on. |
| **Pence to pounds**<br>Change pence into pounds and pence notation. | Solve problems involving addition, subtraction, multiplication or division in contexts of numbers, measures or pounds and pence | **Before:** Revise pence to pounds and pence notation with the class before you give out this homework.<br>**After:** Write some amounts of pence on the board (for example, 345p) and invite children to write them in pounds and pence. Ask them to explain how they worked out the additions. |
| **Nature trail**<br>Read scales on measuring instruments. | Estimate, compare and measure lengths, weights and capacities, choosing and using standard units (m, cm, kg, litre) and suitable measuring instruments | **Before:** Discuss units of measurement and which units we use to measure length, mass and capacity.<br>**After:** Go through the answers with the class. |
| **D2** | | |
| **Telling the time**<br>Read and record times on analogue and digital clocks. | Use units of time (seconds, minutes, hours, days) and know the relationship between them; read the time to the quarter hour | **Before:** Tell the children that they will be reading the time on analogue clock faces and matching it to digital displays.<br>**After:** Check the children's answers to the questions on the worksheet together. |
| **Where is the arrow?**<br>Match words to directions. | Follow and give instructions involving position, direction and movement | **Before:** Show the children the activity sheet and read through the positional and directional language together.<br>**After:** Review the activity, asking some of the children who did the challenge activity to share examples of their work. |
| **Position, direction or movement?**<br>Sort vocabulary of position, direction and movement. | Follow and give instructions involving position, direction and movement | **Before:** Explain that this homework concentrates on vocabulary related to position, direction and movement. The children have to link each word to its appropriate box.<br>**After:** Review the activity as a class. Draw the three 'boxes' on the board. Call out the words and ask the children to say where they go. Encourage the children to make up a sentence using each word, to make sure they have understood it properly. |

## Calculating, measuring and understanding shape

| Activity | Learning objectives | Managing the homework |
|---|---|---|
| **Robo-dog**<br>Give instructions to move Robo-dog around a grid. | Recognise and use whole, half and quarter turns, both clockwise and anticlockwise; know that a right angle represents a quarter turn | **Before:** Revise the vocabulary of movement the children are being asked to use. According to children's ability, you might like to suggest that they try to rescue either one, two or three people in the maze.<br>**After:** Compare answers with the class. Was every child successful? Recap on the relevant movement vocabulary. |
| **D3** | | |
| **Time crossword**<br>Complete a crossword to reinforce vocabulary of time. | Use units of time (seconds, minutes, hours, days) and know the relationship between them | **Before:** Discuss the meaning of the words in the box, asking for possible answers to the clues. You may wish to fill in some of the letters in each word, to make it easier for some children.<br>**After:** Say each solution word and ask the children to make up a clue of their own to demonstrate their understanding of the meanings of the words. |
| **Can you find my partner?**<br>Play a card-matching game to revise vocabulary of time. | Use units of time (seconds, minutes, hours, days) and know the relationship between them | **Before:** Model how to play the game about times of the day, week and year.<br>**After:** Hold up the cards and ask the children to think of a different description of the same time. Ask them to explain their thinking. |
| **Match the time**<br>Play a card-matching game with clock pictures and digital times. | Read the time to the quarter hour | **Before:** Model how to play the game. This game gives children practice in reading the time on analogue and digital clocks.<br>**After:** Hold up the clock faces. Ask the children to write down the digital time and explain their answer. |
| **How fast?**<br>Read the speeds shown on speedometers. | Read the numbered divisions on a scale, and interpret the divisions between them (for example, on a scale from 0 to 25 with intervals of 1 shown but only the divisions 0, 5, 10, 15 and 20 numbered) | **Before:** Discuss the scales used on measuring instruments.<br>**After:** Show another example of a measuring instrument that requires the user to read between the divisions (for example, a wall clock). |

Name Date

# Time for snap!

| | | |
|---|---|---|
| 60 seconds | 1 minute | 1 minute |
| 60 seconds | 1 hour | 60 seconds |
| 24 hours | 1 day | 1 hour |
| 7 days | 1 week | 60 minutes |
| 2 weeks | 1 fortnight | 1 day |
| 52 weeks | 1 year | 24 hours |
| 120 seconds | 2 minutes | 7 days |
| 1 week | 120 seconds | 2 minutes |

**Dear Helper**

This game will help to consolidate your child's learning on units of time. Cut out, shuffle and deal the cards out equally. Place them face down in front of you and take turns to turn a card over from your own pile. If a card shows the same amount of time as the previous card (for example, '1 minute' and '60 seconds') both players should shout 'Snap!'. The first to shout collects the cards. If your child has difficulty, write out the equivalent times on paper for them to refer to. For a challenge, time the children to see how quickly they can link similar cards together.

BLOCK D

Name Date

# Which method?

- Choose from these strategies to work out the calculations.

| Near doubles | Partitioning the last number | Rounding and adjusting |
|---|---|---|
| Counting on | | Number bonds |

Calculation:

Strategy:

Answer:

Calculation:

Strategy:

Answer:

Calculation:

Strategy:

Answer:

Calculation:

Strategy:

Answer:

Calculation:

Strategy:

Answer:

Calculation:

Strategy:

Answer:

Calculation:

Strategy:

Answer:

Calculation:

Strategy:

Answer:

**Dear Helper**

Your child has been learning to add and subtract using different strategies. In this activity, they will need to choose the best strategy to solve different calculations. Please ask your child to explain their choice of strategy to you. The calculations have been specially chosen to match your child's knowledge and understanding of these strategies.

Name Date

# Pence to pounds

- Look at the numbers below. For each example, convert the number of pence into pounds and pence.

| | | | | | |
|---|---|---|---|---|---|
| 125p | → | £1.25 | 302p | → | £3.02 |
| 175p | → | | 345p | → | |
| 225p | → | | 269p | → | |
| 180p | → | | 199p | → | |

- Now add these amounts together and write the answers in pounds and pence.

| | | |
|---|---|---|
| 50p + 80p | 60p + 90p | 70p + 80p |
| 50p + 70p | 75p + 80p | 75p + 75p |

**Dear Helper**

This activity will help your child to practise changing large numbers of pence to pounds and pence. Please provide help as necessary. The first examples have been done for you. If your child has difficulty, they should complete only the first part of this activity. If your child needs a challenge, encourage them to make up and add extra two-digit pence numbers to those in each question.

Name Date

# Nature trail

- Otter Class have been on a nature trail.
- They measured a number of things using different measuring instruments.

- Read the scales and write the correct measurement under each one.

**Dear Helper**

This activity helps your child to estimate, compare and measure lengths, weights and capacities (volumes). The kitchen is an ideal place to practise these skills. Cooking with your child develops lots of skills – weighing, measuring, reading scales and working out quantities, to name just a few.

Name Date

# Telling the time

- Draw lines to connect the matching analogue and digital times.

| | | | |
|---|---|---|---|
|  | 2:30 |  | 3:15 |
| 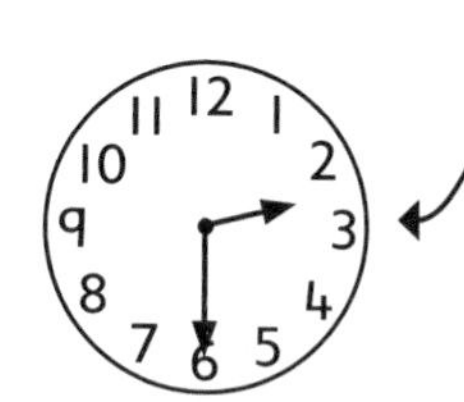 | 9:00 |  | 8:30 |
|  | 4:15 |  | 6:30 |
|  | 7:45 |  | 10:00 |
|  | 5:30 |  | 11:15 |
|  | 1:00 |  | 12:45 |

**Dear Helper**

This activity will help to develop your child's skills in telling the time. Encourage your child to draw lines to match the times on the analogue clock faces on the left with the correct digital times on the right. If your child struggles, encourage them to focus just on reading the times shown on the analogue clock faces. If they find this activity easy, draw some blank circles on the back of the sheet and ask them to complete the clock faces with their own choice of times, and then to write the corresponding digital labels.

Name Date

# Where is the arrow?

- From the words listed below, choose the best description of the position or direction of each arrow.
- Write your answer beneath each box.

| clockwise | anticlockwise | quarter turn |
|---|---|---|
| in front | right angle | above |
| below | behind | beside |

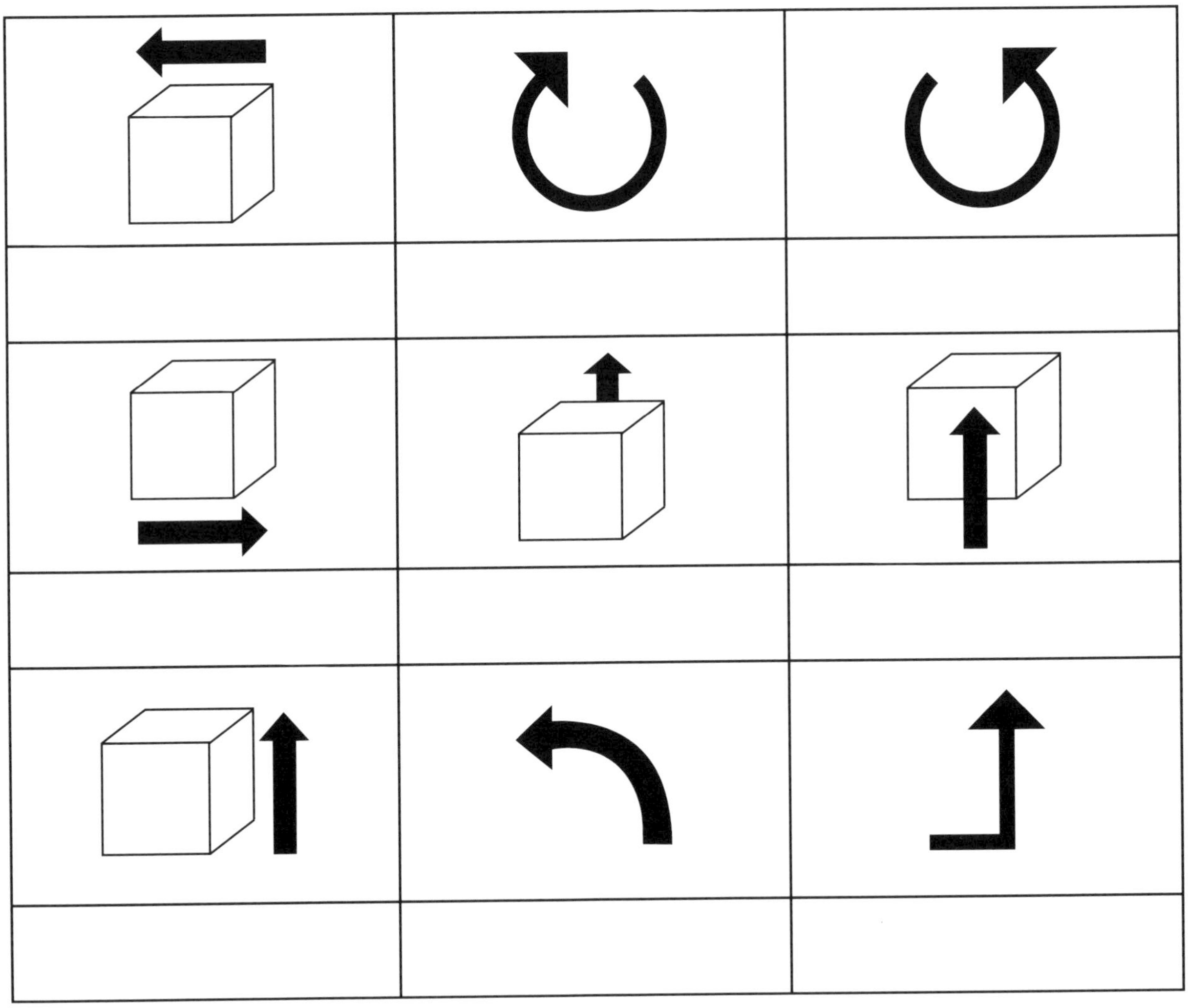

**Dear Helper**
This activity will help consolidate your child's knowledge on position and direction. Discuss the position or direction of the arrow in each picture, and help your child to find the correct word from those listed. Write the answer below each picture. If your child has difficulty, use practical apparatus like a teddy and a box and place the teddy in the positions of the arrows on the sheet. For a challenge, ask your child to think of other positions and direction words and draw arrows to show them.

Name Date

# Position, direction or movement?

- Draw lines to match the vocabulary to its correct box depending on whether it describes a position, direction or movement.

**Position words**

**Direction words**

**Movement words**

clockwise
under
anticlockwise
slide
corner
outside
right
quarter turn
towards
right angle
straight line
backwards
higher
lower
across
front
back
beside
sideways
middle
left
roll



**Dear Helper**

Encourage your child to look at the words above. Help them to match the vocabulary associated with position, direction or movement, to the correct boxes. If your child would like a challenge, ask them to make up a story using some of these words. If your child has difficulty, try to work out the specific words they need to practise and then reinforce these with them.

Name Date

# Robo-dog

- Professor Hatszof has invented a robo-rescue dog.
- Program Robo-dog to rescue the trapped survivors after an earthquake. Robo-dog must rescue the girl first, then the man and then the boy. Then he needs to lead them all back to the tunnel entrance.
- Starting at the tunnel entrance, give Robo-dog his commands and write these down.

HELPFUL HINTS: You can only move in straight lines, forwards and backwards. Remember, Robo-dog cannot move diagonally or through any rocks in the tunnel. You must find a different route avoiding rocks! You need to explain carefully what direction Robo-dog should travel in. For example: *Move forward two squares. Make a quarter turn clockwise.* Remember: a right angle is a quarter turn.

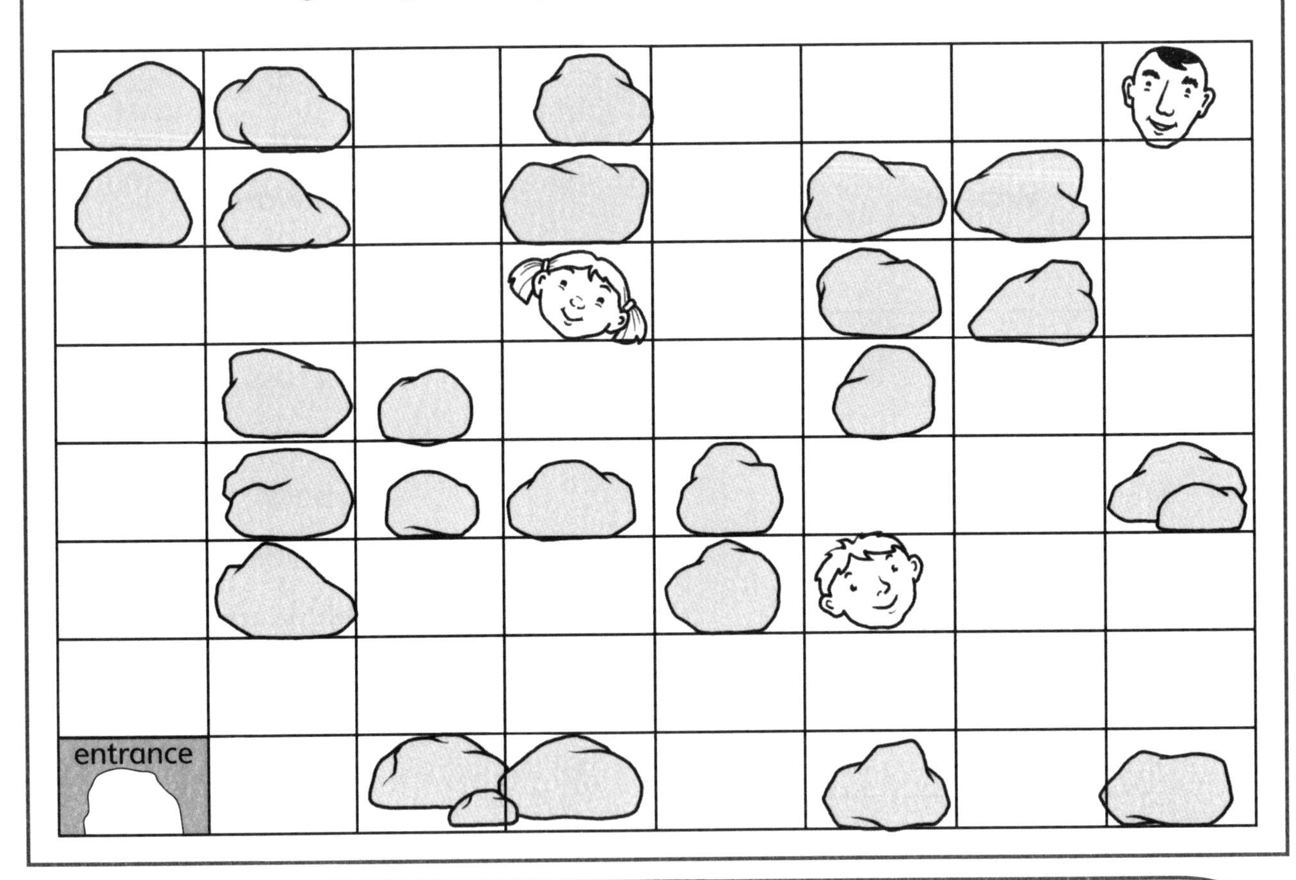


**Dear Helper**

This activity will help your child recognise and use the terms 'anticlockwise', 'clockwise', 'half turn' and 'quarter turn', which they should be familiar with from their lessons at school. Encourage your child to work methodically. You may wish to trace a path through first (or use a counter) to demonstrate the route. Your child could write the instructions for Robo-dog's movements on another piece of paper.

Name Date

# Time crossword

**Words**

morning
minute
fortnight
analogue
after
watch
afternoon
seconds
digital
early
evenings
late

### Clues across

**2.** The time of day when we get up.

**4.** Not before.

**5.** After lunch and before tea.

**7.** Not late.

**9.** Opposite of early.

**10.** The time of the day when we go to bed.

**11.** The type of watch that has just numbers.

### Clues down

**1.** Two weeks.

**3.** We use this to tell the time.

**4.** The type of watch that has hands.

**6.** There are 60 of these in a minute.

**8.** There are 60 of these in an hour.

**Dear Helper**

This activity will help your child to practise some of the vocabulary of time that they have been learning in class. If your child would like a challenge, hide the box with words to choose from. If they need more support, help them by filling in two or three of the answers.

Name Date

# Can you find my partner?

| | | |
|---|---|---|
| Yesterday | The day before today | 60 minutes |
| Hour | Week | Seven days |
| Month | Between four and five weeks | Fortnight |
| Two weeks | Monday to Friday | Weekdays |
| Wednesday | The day before Thursday | Morning |
| Before midday | Tomorrow | The day after today |
| Yesterday | The day before today | Friday |
| The day after Thursday | April | The month before May |
| November | The month after October | 60 seconds |
| 1 minute | Saturday and Sunday | The weekend |

**Dear Helper**
This game will reinforce your child's understanding of measurements of time. Cut out the word cards and place them face down. The first player should turn over two cards. If the cards show the same amount of time (for example, 'Week' and 'Seven days'), the player keeps them. If they do not match, the player should turn them over again and let the next player take a turn. The winner is the player with the most pairs. If your child has difficulty, play with the cards facing up. For a challenge, ask your child to make up a sentence using one of the words they have matched before keeping it.

Name Date

# Match the time

| | | | |
|---|---|---|---|
| 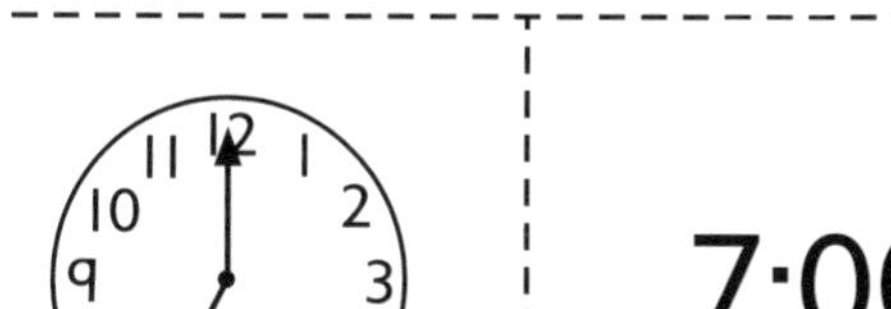 | 7:00 | | 2:30 |
| | 1:15 | | 3:45 |
| | 10:00 |  | 6:30 |
|  | 7:15 |  | 4:45 |
|  | 3:00 |  | 11:30 |

**Dear Helper**

This activity will help your child to read the time on both analogue and digital clocks. Cut out the cards and place them face down. The first player should turn over two cards. If the cards show the same time in analogue and digital format, then the player keeps those cards. If they do not show the same time, the player should turn them over again and let the next player take a turn. The winner is the player with the most pairs. If your child has difficulty, play the game with the cards face up. For a challenge, ask them to make a sentence using one of the words they have matched before keeping it.

Name Date

# How fast?

- These are the speedometers on different bikes in a bike race.
- How fast is each bike going?

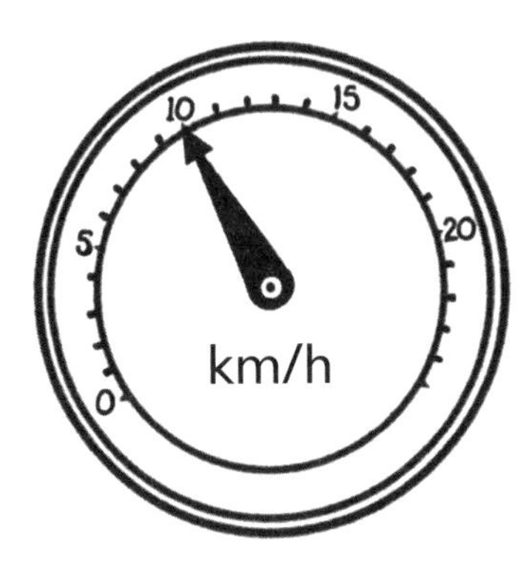


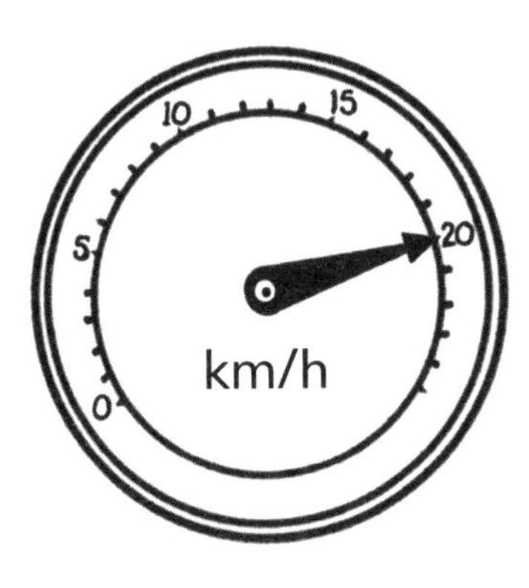


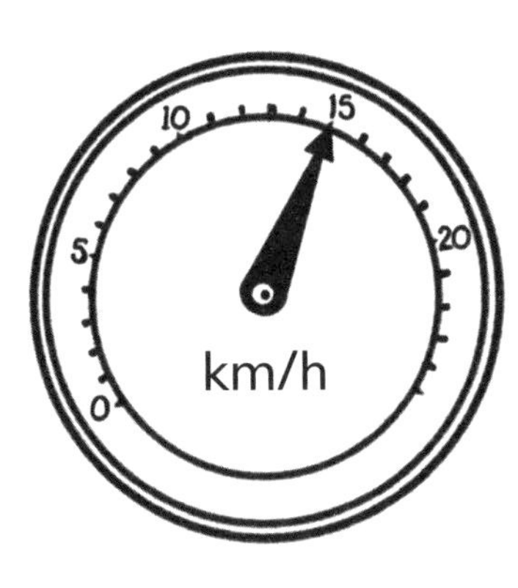


**1** ____________ **2** ____________ **3** ____________

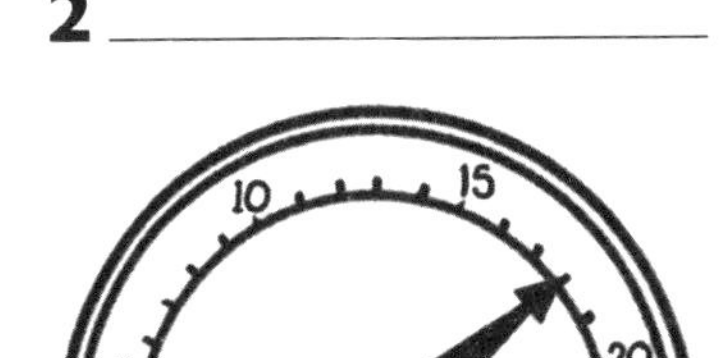

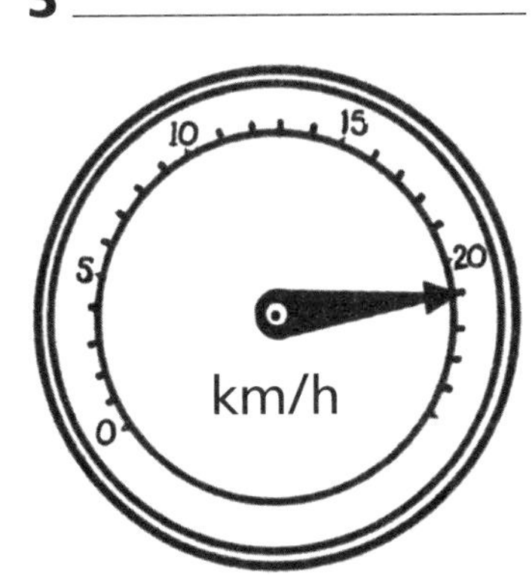


**4** ____________ **5** ____________ **6** ____________

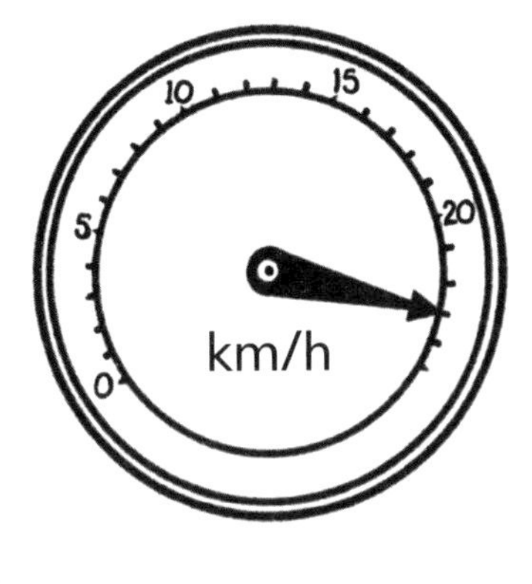


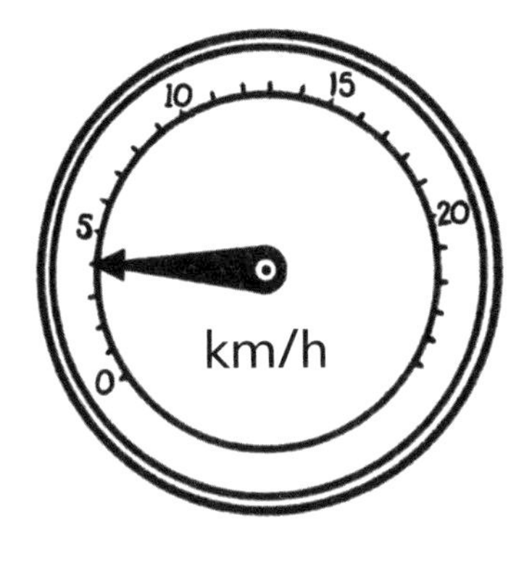


**7** ____________ **8** ____________

**Dear Helper**

This activity helps your child to read and interpret divisions on scales. For more practice, you can also look at dials and displays on a car dashboard. When the car is stationary, show your child all the dials and talk about what they tell the driver. On your next car journey, ask your child if they can read the speedometer and any other dials that are easy to see from their seating position.

| Activity | Learning objectives | Managing the homework |
|---|---|---|
| **E1** | | |
| **Loopy lines**<br>Show multiplication and its inverse by making jumps along a number line. | Represent repeated addition and arrays as multiplication, and sharing and repeated subtraction (grouping) as division; use practical and informal written methods and related vocabulary to support multiplication and division | **Before:** Explain that this activity focuses on multiplication as repeated addition and division as repeated subtraction. Fill in the boxes according to each child's ability.<br>**After:** Work through a few of the children's calculations. Through discussion and self-assessment, check that they understand that division is the opposite operation to multiplication and is repeated subtraction. |
| **Quarter mastery**<br>Use a paper-folding activity to find quarters of shapes. | Find one quarter of shapes | **Before:** Tell the children that this activity involves finding halves and then quarters of different shapes by folding them.<br>**After:** Discuss which shapes could be folded into quarters and which could not, and why. |
| **Percy's hungry**<br>Play a game to practise finding halves and quarters of numbers. | Find one half and one quarter of sets of objects | **Before:** Tell the children that this game requires them to halve and quarter numbers. Fill in the number spinner with appropriate numbers for each child/ability group.<br>**After:** Find out whether the children can correctly work out ½ and ¼ of the numbers that you put on the spinners. |
| **Investigate these facts**<br>Work out word problems involving multiplication and division. | Identify and record the information or calculation needed to solve a puzzle or problem; carry out the steps or calculations and check the solution in the context of the problem | **Before:** Fill in the boxes according to the children's ability. Use numbers ≥20 for less able children, ≥30 for the main group and ≥50 for more able children.<br>**After:** Discuss the children's answers and ask them to explain how they got them. |
| **Bridging 10**<br>Play a game that involves adding numbers by bridging through 10. | Identify and record the information or calculation needed to solve a puzzle or problem; carry out the steps or calculations and check the solution in the context of the problem | **Before:** Tell the children that they will be practising adding 9 or 11 by bridging through 10. Play the game as a class.<br>**After:** Give the children a two-digit number (for example, 48). Ask: *How you would add 9? How would you add 11?* |
| **Equivalents**<br>Name fractions and match equivalent fraction cards. | Find one half, one quarter and three quarters of shapes | **Before:** Use an OHT copy of the worksheet to explain the homework to the children.<br>**After:** Using the OHT, help the children to mark their own work. Ask: *How many quarters make one whole? How many quarters make one half? If we add ½ and ¼, what fraction is that?* |
| **E2** | | |
| **Spotting multiples**<br>Identify multiples of 2, 5 and 10. | Derive and recall multiplication facts for the 2-, 5- and 10-times tables; recognise multiples of 2, 5 and 10 | **Before:** Explain to the children that the homework focuses on multiples of 2, 5 and 10. Rehearse counting in multiples of these numbers.<br>**After:** Correct the activity as a class. Ask: *How do you know that 4 is a multiple of 2 only, 15 is a multiple of 5 only, and 10 is a multiple of 2, 5 and 10?* |
| **Spider charts**<br>Practise 2- and 10-times tables and division facts using spider charts. | Derive and recall multiplication facts for the 2-, 5- and 10-times tables and the related division facts; recognise multiples of 2, 5 and 10 | **Before:** Tell the children that they will be practising their 2- and 10-times tables and will need to ask their helpers to time them.<br>**After:** Ask the children to show if they felt they answered their homework facts quickly. Use an OHT copy of the sheet to practise the tables. |
| **All the same value**<br>Find different multiples of 10p that total £2. | Identify and record the information or calculation needed to solve a puzzle or problem; carry out the steps or calculations and check the solution in the context of the problem | **Before:** Model an example: *The price of all the toys is the same and must be a multiple of 10p. I buy two toys and the total cost is less than £1. How much could they cost?* Work through all the possibilities.<br>**After:** Ask for all the possible answers. Ask: *Could the toys cost 25p each? Why not? Could they cost 80p each? Why not?* |

## Securing number facts, relationships and calculating

| Activity | Learning objectives | Managing the homework |
|---|---|---|
| **Grouping**<br>Use grouping to solve division problems. | Represent sharing and repeated subtraction (grouping) as division; use practical and informal written methods and related vocabulary to support division | **Before:** Fill in the numbers according to the children's ability. Work through a couple of examples.<br>**After:** Determine whether the children understand grouping by working out some calculations together. |
| **Halves and quarters**<br>Play a game of halves and quarters. | Find one half and one quarter of sets of objects | **Before:** Ensure that the children understand what halves and quarters are in the context of a small number of objects.<br>**After:** Repeat the game, playing against the class. Ask the children how they find a quarter or a half. Do they partition or keep the number whole? Do they use the halving facts that they have learned in school? |
| **Mixed bag of problems**<br>Solve a range of word problems. | Solve problems involving addition, subtraction, multiplication or division in contexts of numbers, measures or pounds and pence | **Before:** Encourage the children to read the questions carefully and more than once.<br>**After:** Discuss how they decided which operation to use before each calculation. |
| **E3** | | |
| **How many ways?**<br>Find ways of making a given number. | Present solutions to puzzles and problems in an organised way; explain decisions, methods and results in pictorial, spoken or written form, using mathematical language and number sentences | **Before:** Fill in the numbers you want the children to make. Multiples of 3, 4 and/or 5 will be useful to elicit times-table facts.<br>**After:** Using an OHT of the sheet, invite some children to share their work. Ask the others to add their own ideas; encourage them to suggest any operations that have not yet been used. |
| **Fraction problems**<br>Solve fraction problems involving different operations. | • Identify and record the information or calculation needed to solve a puzzle or problem; carry out the steps or calculations and check the solution in the context of the problem<br>• Find one half, one quarter and three quarters of shapes and sets of objects | **Before:** Fill in appropriate numbers to differentiate the sheets.<br>**After:** Go through the homework with each group, so they can mark their own work. Ask questions such as: *What did you need to find out? What fraction were you trying to find? How did you work it out? Does your answer seem right?* |
| **What's the difference between...?**<br>Find the difference between two numbers. | • Solve problems involving subtraction<br>• Explain results using mathematical language and number sentences | **Before:** Discuss the language used relating to subtraction.<br>**After:** Go through the answers with the class and recap on the vocabulary used. |
| **Magic Mike**<br>Find the unknown numbers in number sentences. | Calculate the value of an unknown in a number sentence | **Before:** Show an example of a complete number sentence and an example with an unknown value.<br>**After:** Go through the answers with the class and discuss the methods the children used to answer the questions. Did anyone use inverse operations? |
| **Dartboards**<br>Double and halve numbers up to 20. | Understand that halving is the inverse of doubling and derive and recall doubles of all numbers to 20, and the corresponding halves | **Before:** Discuss the vocabulary of doubles and halves.<br>**After:** Discuss doubling and halving as multiplying and dividing by 2. |
| **Friendly number quiz**<br>2-, 5- and 10-times tables test. | Recall multiplication facts for the 2-, 5- and 10-times tables and the related division facts; recognise multiples of 2, 5 and 10 | **Before:** Revise the 2-, 5- and 10-times tables.<br>**After:** Do a quick-fire quiz with the class on the 2-, 5- and 10-times tables. |

BLOCK E

Name Date

# Loopy lines

- Complete the number lines by drawing loops along the lines to show the multiplication or division in each box.
- Write your calculation and the answer underneath each number line.

2 × 5

0 1 2 3 4 5 6 7 8 9 10

+ 2 + 2 + 2 + 2 + 2

2 + 2 + 2 + 2 + 2 = 10

0 1 2 3 4 5 6 7 8 9 10 11 12 13 14 15 16 17 18 19 20

0 1 2 3 4 5 6 7 8 9 10 11 12 13 14 15 16 17 18 19 20

0 1 2 3 4 5 6 7 8 9 10 11 12 13 14 15 16 17 18 19 20

0 1 2 3 4 5 6 7 8 9 10 11 12 13 14 15 16 17 18 19 20

**Dear Helper**

Your child has been learning that division is repeated subtraction. Remind them that this is the opposite of multiplication, which is repeated addition. Work through the examples with your child. Encourage your child to write the repeated addition or subtraction, and the answer, underneath each number line (see example at top of page). The multiplications/divisions have been chosen according to your child's confidence with multiplication/division.

Name Date

# Quarter mastery

- Cut out each shape and fold it into four quarters.
- Unfold the shape and mark along the fold lines with a coloured pen.
- Which shapes have four identical sections?

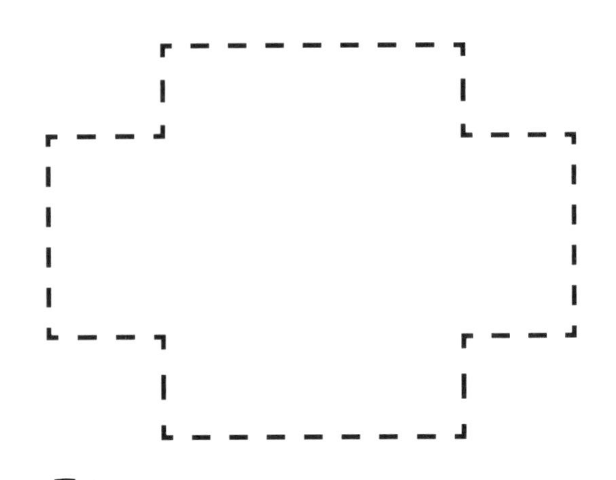

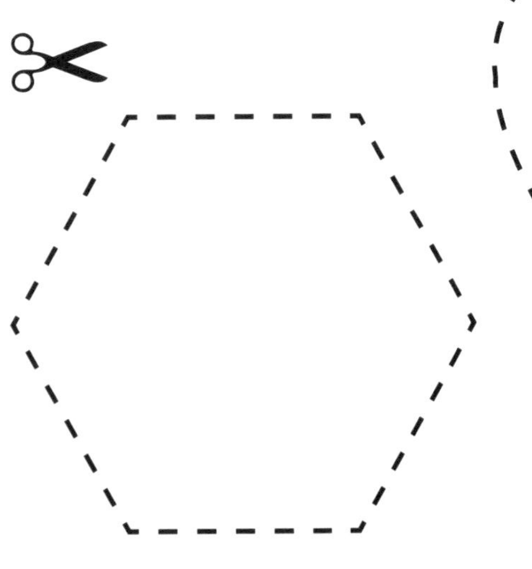

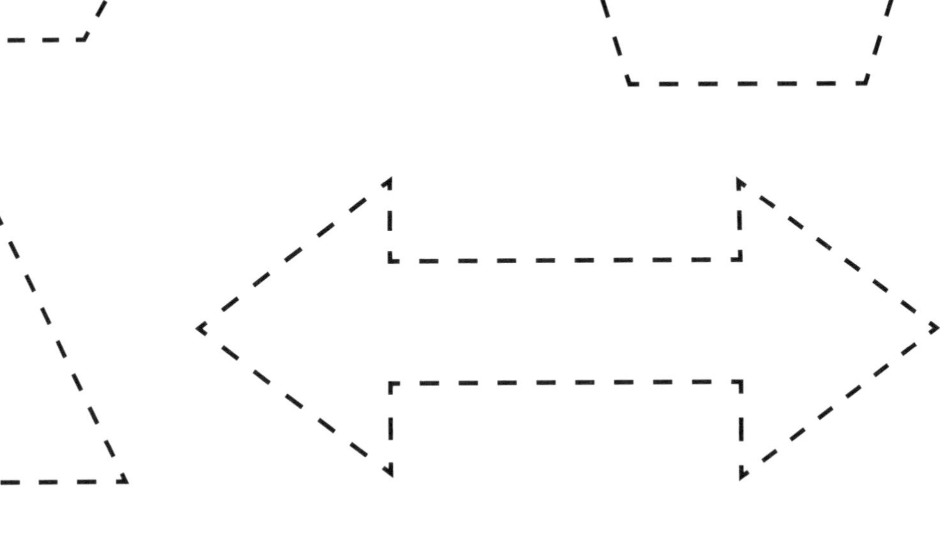

**Dear Helper**

This activity will consolidate the work that your child has been doing on fractions and shapes. Help your child to carefully cut out each shape, then challenge them to fold each shape into quarters. Ask your child to unfold their shapes and mark along the fold lines. On a separate piece of paper, encourage your child to record which of the shapes are formed from four identical quarters.

Name Date

# Percy's hungry

- Cut out each spinner. Put the sharp end of a pencil through a paper clip and then through the middle of the spinner.
- Spin the paper clip around the fraction spinner.
- Spin the paper clip around the number spinner.
- Work out the answer to the fraction sum and place that amount of counters on Percy's tummy.

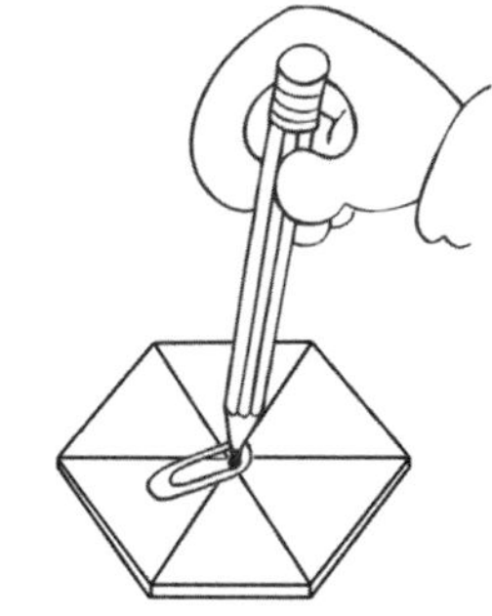

**Number spinner**

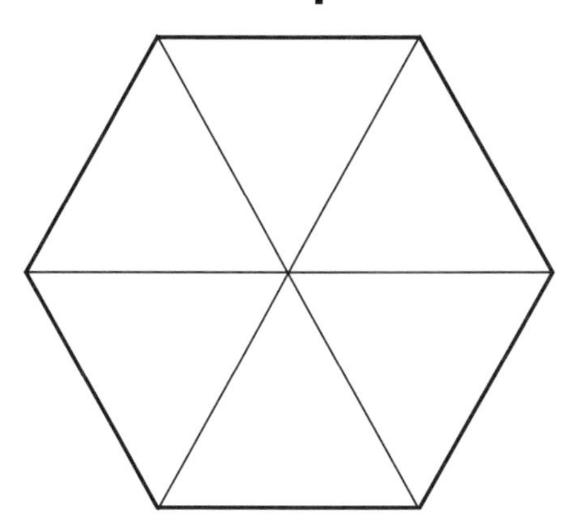

**Fraction spinner**

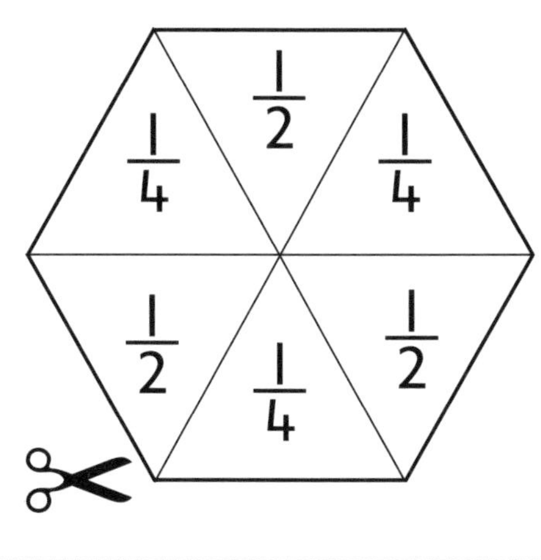

**Dear Helper**

This game will help your child to work out halves and quarters of numbers. The numbers on the number spinner have been specifically chosen for your child. You will need some buttons or counters to represent food for Percy. Encourage your child to flick the paper clip around the fraction spinner to choose a fraction, and around the number spinner to choose a number. Help your child to work out the answer depending on the numbers spun. So, for example, if they spin a quarter and 12, then they must work out one quarter of 12, and count out that many counters to put on to Percy's tummy. How much food can your child feed Percy in five minutes?

Name Date

# Investigate these facts

A car has 4 wheels.

How many wheels are there on ☐ cars?

______________________

Show how you worked this out.

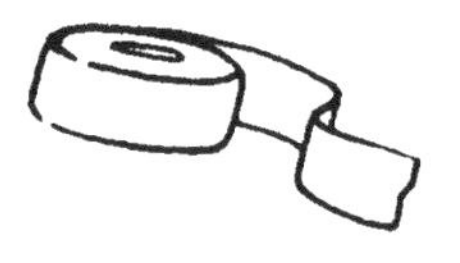

Sara had ☐ cm of sticky tape.

She wanted to cut it into ☐ cm lengths.

How many lengths can she cut? ____________

Show how you worked this out.

Jo had a ☐ m length of rope.

Sam had ☐ times as much.

How much did Sam have? ____________

How much did Jo and Sam have altogether?

______________________

Show how you worked this out.

Emma has ☐ stamps.

Ravi has ☐ stamps for every one of Emma's.

How many stamps does Ravi have?

______________________

Show how you worked this out.

**Dear Helper**

This activity will help your child to practise problem solving that involves multiplication and division. The numbers have been specially chosen to match your child's ability. Please provide help to read the problems if necessary. Your child may find it helpful to use practical objects, such as pennies or pieces of pasta, for this activity. If your child needs a challenge, ask them to make up similar questions for you to answer.

 

Name Date

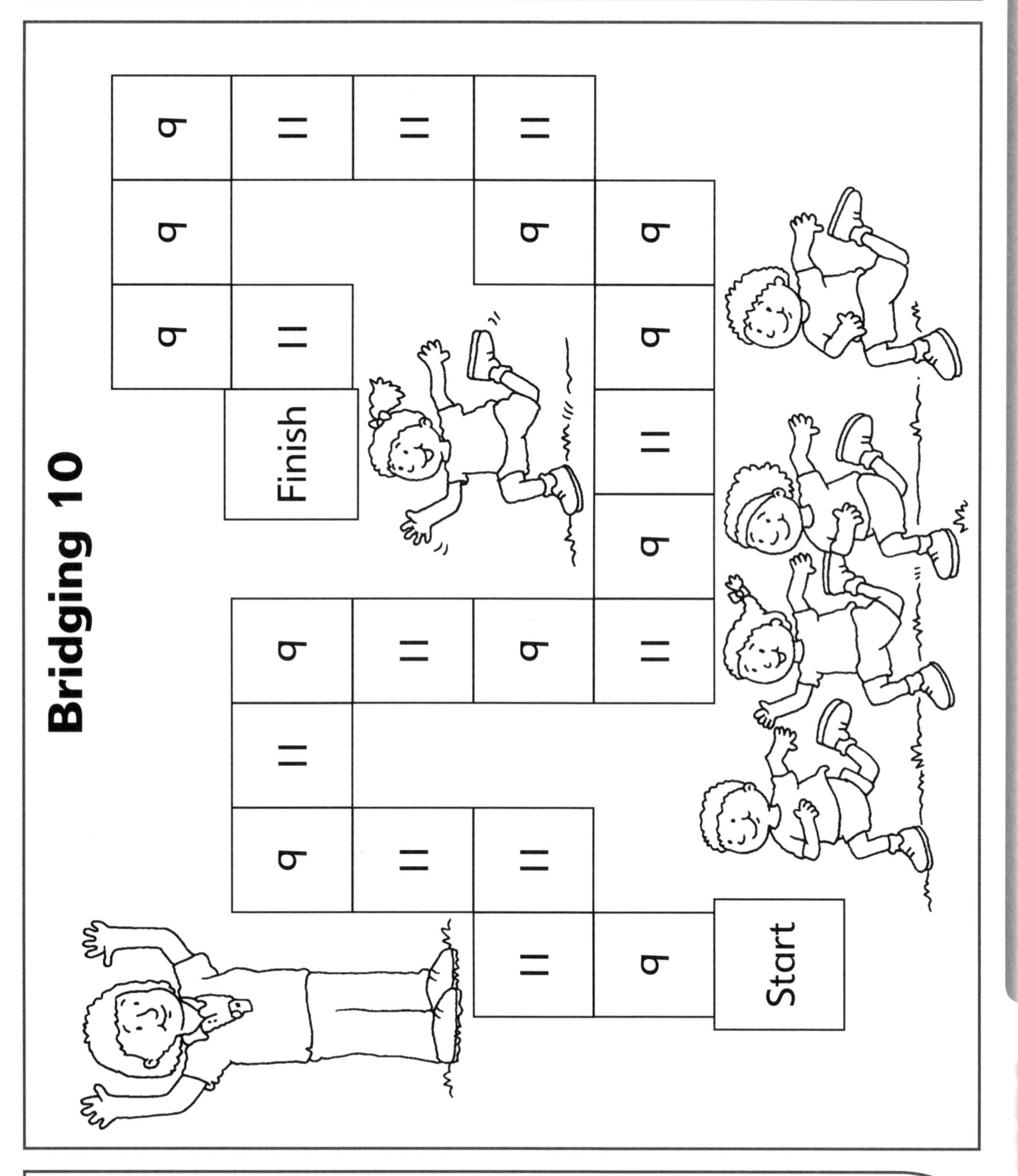


**Dear Helper**

This game will provide practice in adding numbers and adjusting by 1. You will need two dice and a different-coloured counter each. Place your counters on 'Start'. The first player should roll both dice and make the smallest two-digit number they can. Using the first number in the game (9), they should add 9 to their number by adding 10 and taking away 1. They should then move their counter according to the number of tens in their answer. For example, if you throw a 3 and a 6, you would make 36. Add 9 (36 + 10 – 1) to give 45. There are four tens in 45, so move on four spaces to land on 11. On the next go, you would add 11 to your two-digit number (add 10 and then 1). If your child has difficulty, use one dice, adding 9 or 11. For a challenge, ask them to look at the two possible numbers they could make and decide which will allow them to make the most moves.

Name Date

# Equivalents

■ For each shape, match the shaded area to the corresponding fraction.

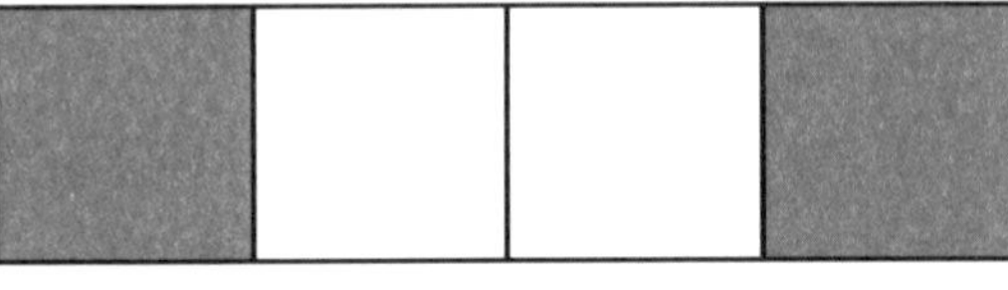
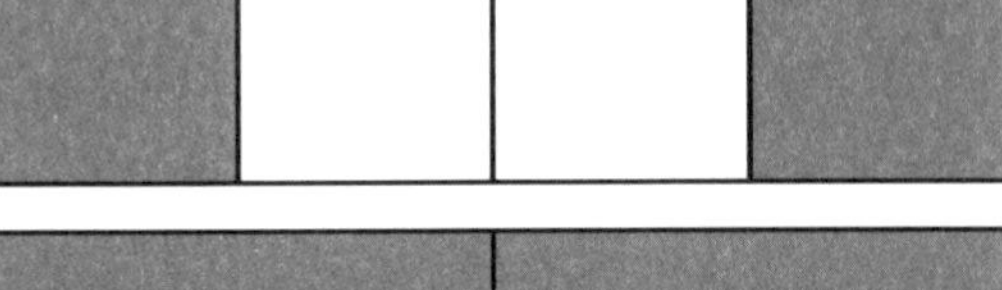
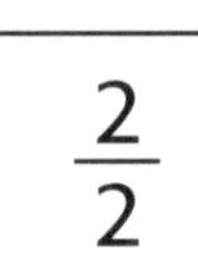
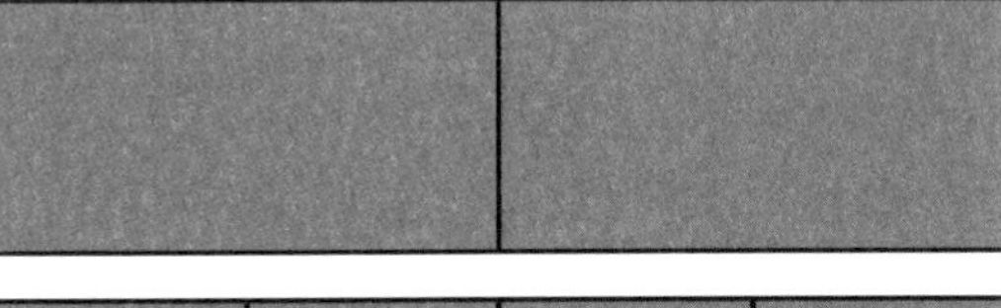
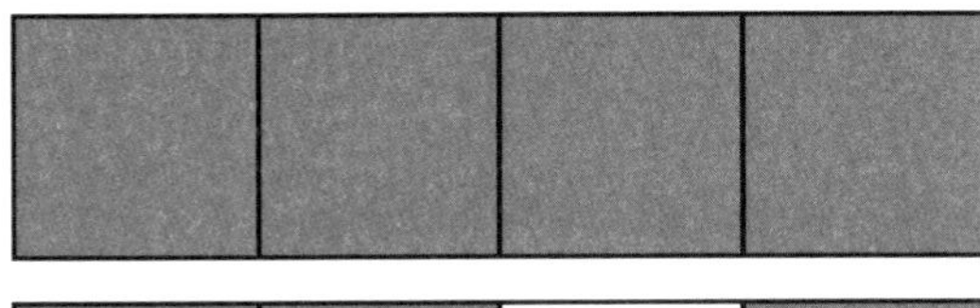
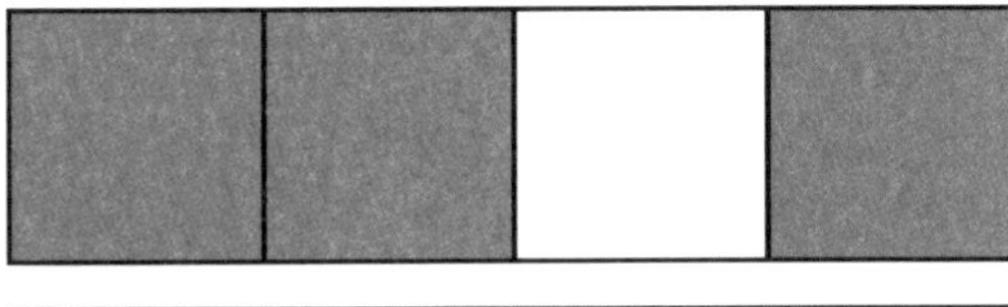
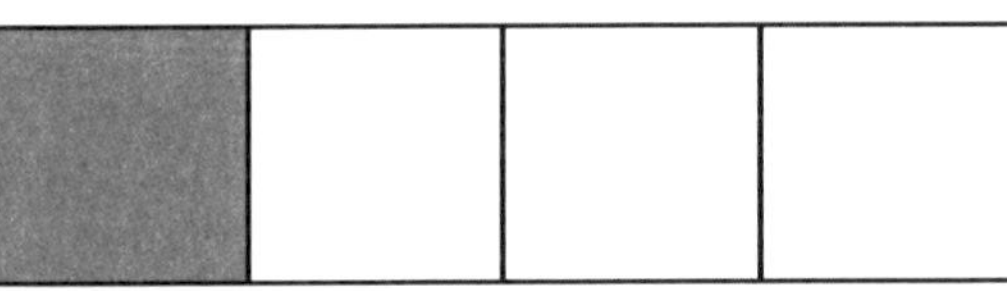

$\frac{2}{2}$

$\frac{1}{2}$

$\frac{1}{4}$

$\frac{2}{4}$

$\frac{4}{4}$

$1$

$\frac{3}{4}$

Number sentences:

$\frac{1}{2} = \square + \square$

1 whole = $\square + \square$

$\frac{3}{4} = \square + \square$

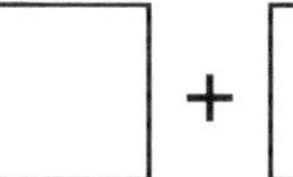

**Dear Helper**

Ask your child to look at each picture, work out the fraction that is shaded, then draw a line to link the shape to the correct matching fraction on the right-hand side of the page. Afterwards, encourage your child to fill in the number sentences at the bottom of the page.

Name Date

# Spotting multiples

- Put a ring around the multiples of 2 on this line:

1 2 3 4 5 6 7 8 9 10 11 12 13 14 15 16 17 18 19 20

- Put a ring around the multiples of 5 on this line:

7 8 9 10 11 12 13 14 15 16 17 18 19 20 21 22 23 24 25

- Put a ring around the multiples of 10 on this line:

9 10 11 12 13 14 15 16 17 18 19 20 21 22 23 24

- Put a ring around the multiples of 2 and a square around the multiples of 5 on this line:

31 32 33 34 35 36 37 38 39 40 41 42 43 44 45 46 47 48 49 50

- Put a ring around the multiples of 5 and a square around the multiples of 10 on this line:

47 48 49 50 51 52 53 54 55 56 57 58 59 60 61 62

- Which of these are multiples of 2? Put a ring around them:

23 44 12 67 43 78 14 16 60 38 21 83 97

- How do you know which numbers are multiples of 2? Write down your answer on the back of the sheet.

**Dear Helper**

This activity will help your child to recognise multiples of 2, 5 and 10. If they have difficulty, concentrate on multiples of one number only. To challenge your child, see if they can make up number lines for three-digit numbers and find different multiples.

Name Date

# Spider charts

Multiplication

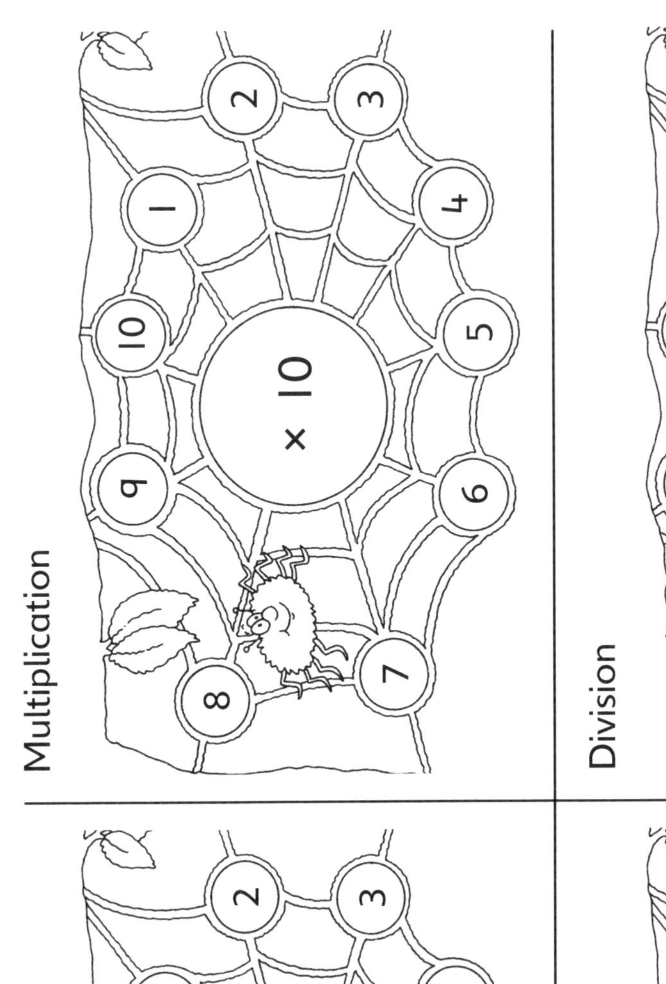


Division

Multiplication

× 2

Division

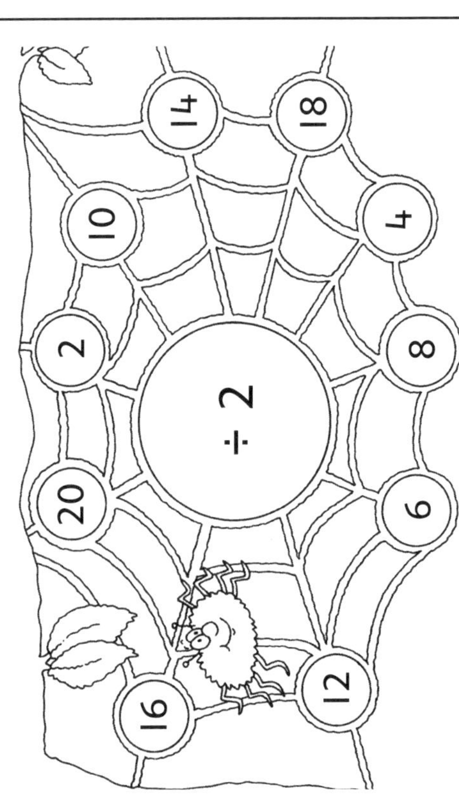


**Dear Helper**

These spider charts will help your child to practise their 2- and 10-times tables. For the multiplication charts, point to a number on the outside of the chart and challenge your child to multiply it by 2 (or 10, depending on which chart you are using) and call out the answer. Time your child to see how quickly they can work out the answer. Do the same with the division charts.

Name Date

# All the same value

- These three toys all cost the same price. The price is a multiple of ten pence. The total cost of the three toys is less than £2. What could the value of each toy be? Write your answers in the box below.

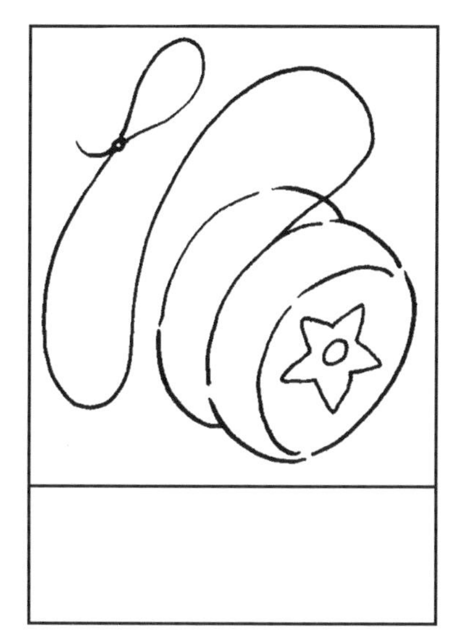

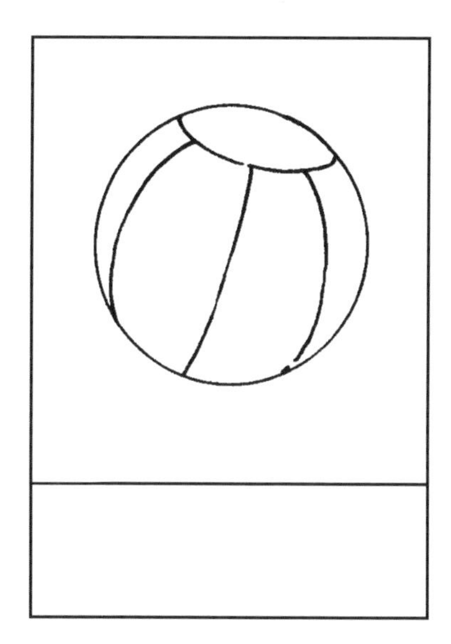

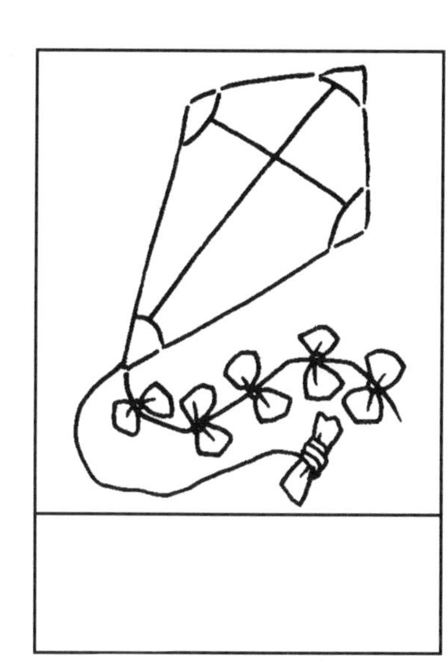

My answers:

- What could the value of each toy be if the total was a multiple of five pence and less than £1?

My answers:

**Dear Helper**
Your child has been investigating number problems and learning that investigations often result in more than one answer. For their homework, your child should find and record all possible answers to the questions above. Encourage your child to be systematic in their approach.

Name Date

# Grouping

■ Work out the following division facts. Use the grouping method to help you.

$8 \div 2$

$8 \xrightarrow{-2} 6 \xrightarrow{-2} 4 \xrightarrow{-2} 2 \xrightarrow{-2} 0$

We can take 4 lots of 2 away from 8, so
$8 \div 2 = 4$

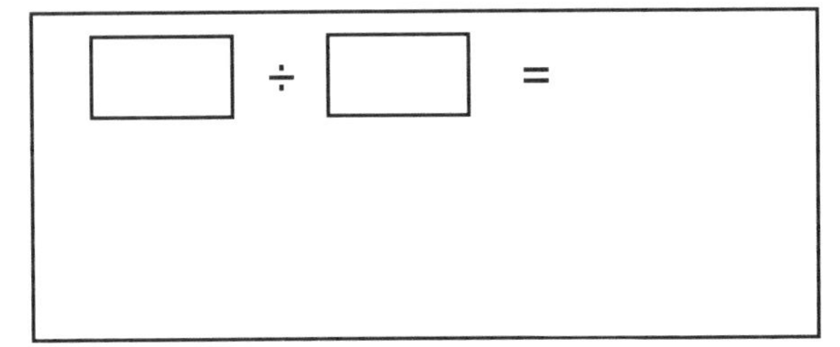

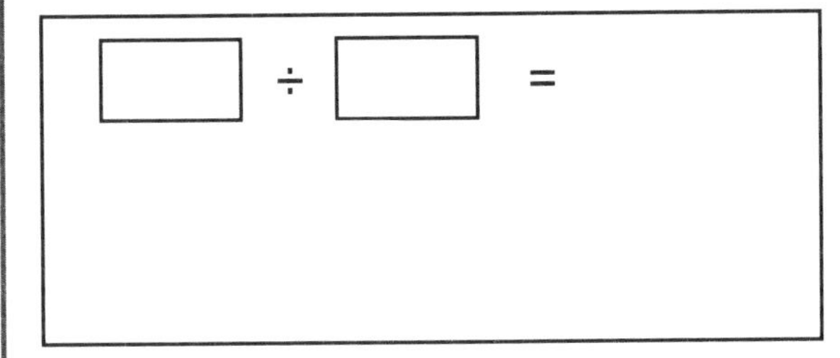

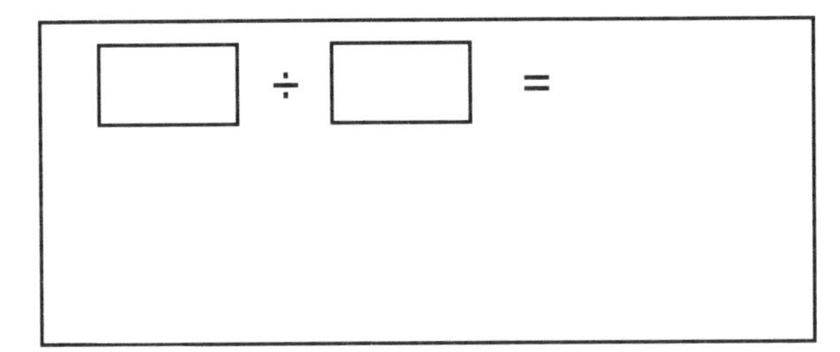

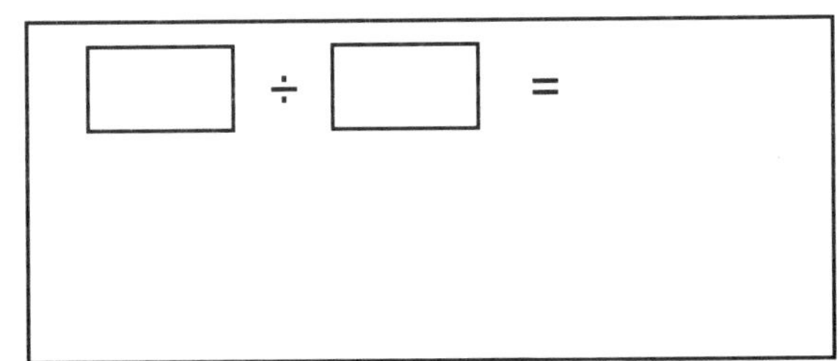

$\square \div \square =$

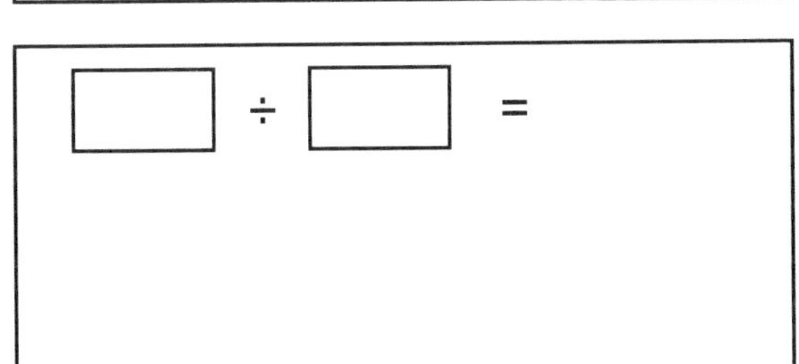

$\square \div \square =$

■ Make up some more of your own on the back of this sheet for your Helper to solve.

**Dear Helper**

This activity will help your child to practise the division work that they have been doing in class. The numbers have been specially chosen for your child. Work through each example together, using the space available in each box to write down the calculations. Encourage your child to find the answers by grouping. For example: 8 ÷ 2. To work this out your child will need to find out how many groups of 2 there are in 8. They can do this by taking groups of 2 away from 8 (see the first example). If your child has difficulty with two-digit examples, ask them just to partition numbers into tens and ones. For a challenge, ask your child to use pairs of two-digit numbers to make up their own calculations.

Name Date

# Halves and quarters

| Amount | $\frac{1}{2}$ | $\frac{1}{4}$ | Points |
|---|---|---|---|
| 8 | 4 | 2 | 6 |
| 15 | No | No | 0 |
| 18 | 9 | No | 2 |

- Drop a handful of counters onto a table. Count how many there are.
- Can you halve this number? Can you quarter this number? Award yourself the correct number of points as shown above.

**Child**

| Amount | $\frac{1}{2}$ | $\frac{1}{4}$ | Points |
|---|---|---|---|
| | | | |
| | | | |
| | | | |
| | | | |
| | | | |
| | | | |
| | | | |
| | | | |
| | | | |
| | | | |

**Helper**

| Amount | $\frac{1}{2}$ | $\frac{1}{4}$ | Points |
|---|---|---|---|
| | | | |
| | | | |
| | | | |
| | | | |
| | | | |
| | | | |
| | | | |
| | | | |
| | | | |
| | | | |

**Dear Helper**

This game will help to consolidate the work on fractions that your child has been doing in class. You will need lots of counters. Encourage your child to start the game by picking up a handful of counters and dropping them onto the table. Can they divide them into half? If they can, they score two points. Can they divide them into quarters? If so, they score four points. For each turn, fill in one row of the table, writing the number of counters dropped and what its half or quarter value is, or 'No' if the fraction is not possible, and the points scored. The first player to score 20 points is the winner. For a challenge, use more counters. If your child has difficulty, play the game concentrating on halves only.

Name Date

# Mixed bag of problems

- Try this mixed bag of 'real-life' problems.

1. Pussykins had 9 kittens. Six were white, the rest were black. How many black kittens were there?

2. I have 18 chocolates. I give you half of them. How many chocolates do you get?

3. I can put 6 toy cars in a box. I have 24 toy cars. How many boxes will I need?

4. Alex had these coins in his moneybox:

Laura gave him a £2 coin. How much does Alex have now?

5. How many 10p coins does Kim need to buy something that costs 97p?

6. I buy 3 apples, 2 pears and a grapefruit. Each label shows the cost per one item of fruit. How much do I spend?

7. One shirt costs £8. Raj buys 5 shirts. How much has Raj spent?

**Dear Helper**
This activity helps your child to solve real-life problems using addition, subtraction, multiplication or division in a variety of contexts. Using money is an excellent, practical way for your child to develop their mathematical skills. Challenge your child to write their own real-life problems for you to answer.

Name Date

# How many ways?

Make

Make

My ways of making this number:

My ways of making this number:

**Dear Helper**

Your child has been investigating ways of making numbers. The numbers in the stars have been chosen specially for your child. Encourage them to find at least 15 different ways to make each number. For example, if the number was 24, they could use some of the following ways: half of 48; 25 – 1; 20 + 4; 10 × 2 + 4; 12 × 2, and so on. If your child is having difficulty, lower the target to ten ways. If your child needs a challenge, ask them to think of interesting and complex ways of reaching the totals.

Name Date

# Fraction problems

Emma saw ☐ lions at the zoo. A quarter of them were very hungry but the rest were not. How many lions were very hungry?

My answer and how I worked it out:

Ravi went to feed the penguins. He was given ☐ fish. He threw half of them in the water and half on to the rocks. How many fish were in the water?

My answer and how I worked it out:

Tom saw ☐ monkeys. A quarter of them were swinging in the trees and the rest were sleeping. How many monkeys were sleeping?

My answer and how I worked it out:

Jade saw ☐ parrots. Half of them were squawking. How many were not squawking?

My answer and how I worked it out:

Oliver saw ☐ turtles. A quarter of them were adult turtles and the rest were baby turtles. How many of them were baby turtles?

My answer and how I worked it out:

**Dear Helper**
This activity will help your child to practise the problem-solving work that they have been doing in class. Help your child to read and answer each problem. The numbers have been specially chosen for your child.

Name Date

# What's the difference between...?

- If you are asked 'What's the difference between these two numbers?', do you know what you have to do?
- You need to take away, or subtract, the smaller number from the larger number.
- Have a go at answering these.
- What is the difference between:

**1.** 12 and 18

**2.** 21 and 7

**3.** 23 and 32

**4.** 16 and 44

**5.** 29 and 38

**6.** 31 and 50

**7.** 47 and 9

**8.** 15 and 33

**Dear Helper**
This activity helps to familiarise your child with the vocabulary of word problems involving subtraction. Children have to learn the vocabulary of maths as well as what all the different symbols mean.

Name Date

# Magic Mike

- Magic Mike has made some of the numbers disappear from these calculations.
- Put the correct numbers back into these number sentences.

26 – 12 =

31 – = 13

– 20 = 24

– 23 = 14

17 – = 13

– 37 = 11

36 – = 24

29 – 17 =

**Dear Helper**

This activity helps your child to find unknown values in number sentences. This can be a difficult activity for some children. If your child does find this difficult, look at different ways to solve the problems. Use cubes or a pencil and paper for 'workings out'. Sometimes drawing the problem on paper can help the child 'see' the answer.

Name Date

# Dartboards

- Dave has made two dartboards but he can't remember all his doubles and halves.
- To help him, write the correct numbers in the outer ring of each board.

**Doubles board**

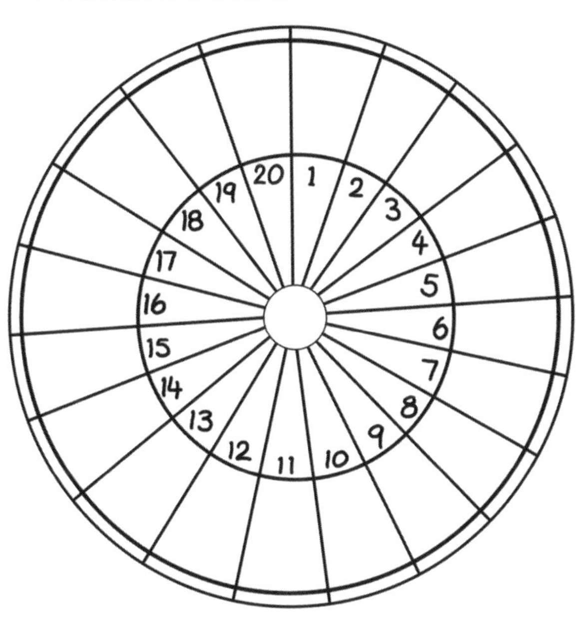

**Halves board**

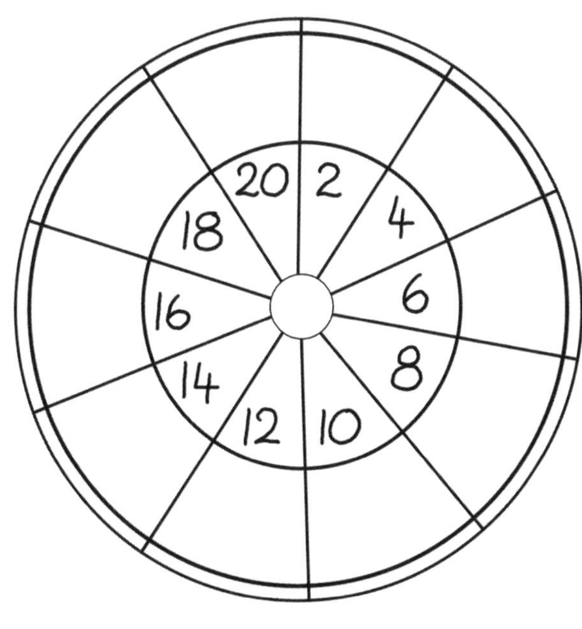


**Dear Helper**
This activity helps your child to learn the doubles and halves of the numbers up to 20. You could try timing your child as an extra challenge. The quicker your child's recall, the better!

Name Date

# Friendly number quiz

- 2, 5 and 10 are friendly numbers because they are the easiest to work with – much easier than difficult numbers like 17 or 13!
- Try this quiz about our friends 2, 5 and 10.

**1.** $5 \times 5 =$ ☐

**2.** $10 \times 4 =$ ☐

**3.** $2 \times 8 =$ ☐

**4.** $5 \times 9 =$ ☐

**5.** $7 \times 10 =$ ☐

**6.** $6 \times 2 =$ ☐

**7.** $10 \div 2 =$ ☐

**8.** $50 \div 10 =$ ☐

**9.** $30 \div 5 =$ ☐

**10.** Circle the number that is a multiple of 2: 33 51 43 28 65

**11.** Circle the number that is a multiple of 5: 12 26 38 45 63

**12.** Circle the number that is a multiple of 10: 11 21 30 46 59

- What's your score? 

**Dear Helper**

This activity helps your child to recall multiplication facts for the 2-, 5- and 10-times tables and the related division facts and to recognise multiples of 2, 5 and 10. It is expected that at the end of Year 2 all children should know the 2-, 5- and 10-times tables, so make sure your child does! Practise over the long summer holiday so they don't get rusty before going into Year 3.

## Puzzles and problems: Objectives grid

The puzzles and problems activities can be used very flexibly to provide children with fun maths tasks to take home. The puzzles and problems are based on work that children will be covering during the year and should test their use and application of mathematics at an appropriate level. Where possible, children should be encouraged to try different approaches to solving these problems and to look for clues and patterns in mathematics.

The grid below lists each activity and identifies links to the different objectives within the Using and applying mathematics strand of the Renewed Framework.

| | Solve problems involving addition, subtraction, multiplication or division in context of numbers, measures or pounds and pence | Identify and record the information or calculation needed to solve a puzzle or problem; carry out the steps or calculations and check the solution in the context of the problem | Follow a line of enquiry; answer questions by choosing and using suitable equipment and selecting, organising and presenting data in lists, tables and simple diagrams | Describe patterns and relationships involving numbers or shapes, make predictions and test these with examples | Present solutions to puzzles and problems in an organised way; explain decisions, methods and results in pictorial, spoken or written form, using mathematical language and number sentences |
|---|---|---|---|---|---|
| **1** Comics | ✔ | | | | |
| **2** Unlucky Ducky | | | | | ✔ |
| **3** Santa's little helper | | ✔ | | | |
| **4** Hopscotch | | | | ✔ | |
| **5** Puzzling pyramid | | | | ✔ | |
| **6** Let's play darts! | ✔ | | | | |
| **7** How long? | | | ✔ | | |
| **8** That's dicey! | ✔ | | | | |
| **9** Take your seats! | | ✔ | | | |
| **10** Where am I heading? | | ✔ | | | |
| **11** Is that the time? | ✔ | | | | |
| **12** 2D mystery shape | | | | ✔ | |
| **13** 3D mystery shape | | | | ✔ | |
| **14** Time to reflect | | | | ✔ | |
| **15** How tall? | | | | | ✔ |
| **16** Homemade jigsaw | | | | ✔ | |
| **17** Stinky Stu | ✔ | | | | |
| **18** Double up | ✔ | | | | |
| **19** Halve it | ✔ | | | | |
| **20** Going bananas | ✔ | | | | |
| **21** Juggler | ✔ | | | | |
| **22** Multi-storey | ✔ | | | | |
| **23** Generous Jenna | ✔ | | | | |
| **24** Guess the weight | | | ✔ | | |
| **25** Balancing act | | | ✔ | | |
| **26** Thirsty work! | | ✔ | | | |
| **27** Coining it | ✔ | | | | |
| **28** Safe-cracker | | | | ✔ | |
| **29** Shady shapes | | | | ✔ | |
| **30** Mixed-up Mickey | | ✔ | | | |
| **31** Guess the amount | | | | ✔ | |
| **32** Pairing-up challenge | ✔ | | | | |
| **33** Flower pots | ✔ | | | | |
| **34** Who am I? | | | | ✔ | |
| **35** How long? | | | ✔ | | |
| **36** What would you use? | | | ✔ | | |

## 1 Comics

Eddie bought a comic for 20p.

He paid for it exactly with silver coins.

There are several different ways he can do it. Can you find them all?

## 2 Unlucky Ducky

Unlucky Ducky is trying to make the number 13 with these cards.

How many different ways could she do it, using number 6 as one of the cards each time?

## 3 Santa's little helper

How many ways can you put the 15 parcels into the three sacks?

Write your answers in this table. Each time, fill the first sack with five parcels.

| Sack 1 | Sack 2 | Sack 3 |
|---|---|---|
| | | |
| | | |
| | | |
| | | |
| | | |

## 4 Hopscotch

Fill in the missing numbers on these hopscotch frames.

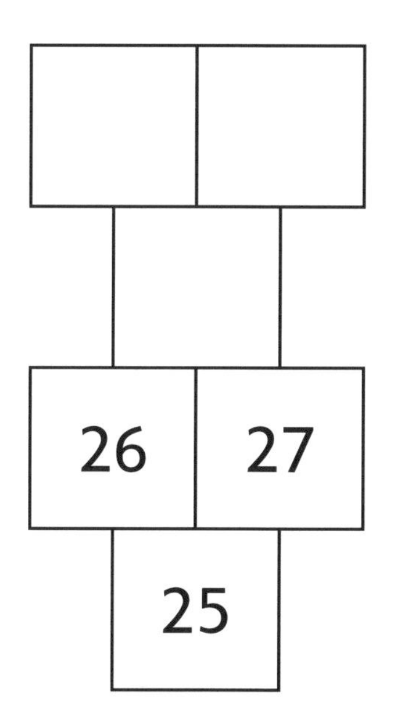


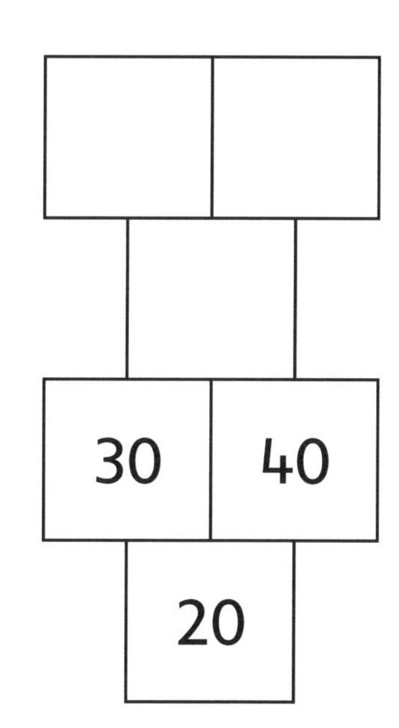


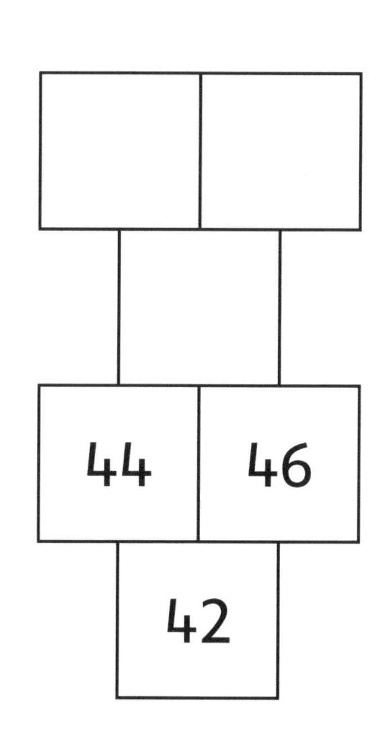

## 5 Puzzling pyramid

How many triangles can you find in this pyramid?

## 6 Let's play darts!

Kanika threw three darts.

More than one dart can go in each score.

What is the highest score Kanika could get?

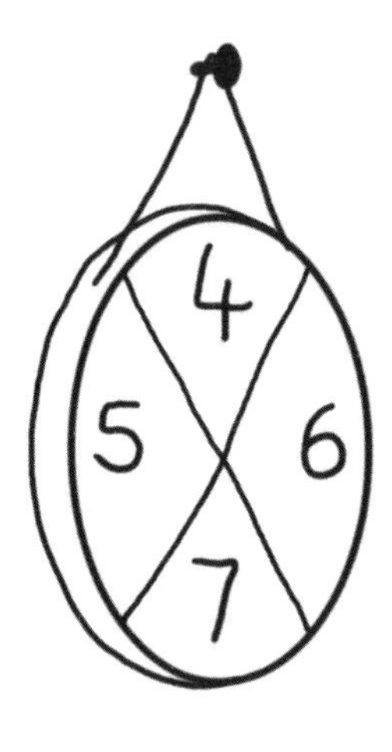

Write all the scores Kanika could get if each dart hit a different number.

## 7 How long?

Use a ruler to measure these slinky snakes to the nearest centimetre.

Snake 1

____________________________

Snake 2

____________________________

## 8 That's dicey!

How many ways can you score 12 by rolling three dice?

____________________________

____________________________

# 9 Take your seats!

Help Charlie arrange these numbered chairs in the correct order – lowest number first.

lowest highest

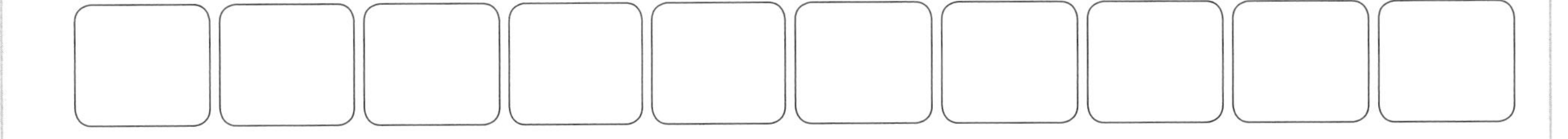

# 10 Where am I heading?

I am facing north.

I take a quarter turn anticlockwise.

Which direction am I facing now?

____________________

## 11 Is that the time?

Rhianna started playing Super Penguin on her console at 6.00pm.

She finished her game $2\frac{1}{2}$ hours later.

At what time did Rhianna finish playing Super Penguin?

______________________

## 12 2D mystery shape

I am a 2D shape.

I have four corners.

I have two sets of sides that are equal in length.

I am not a square.

What am I?

______________________

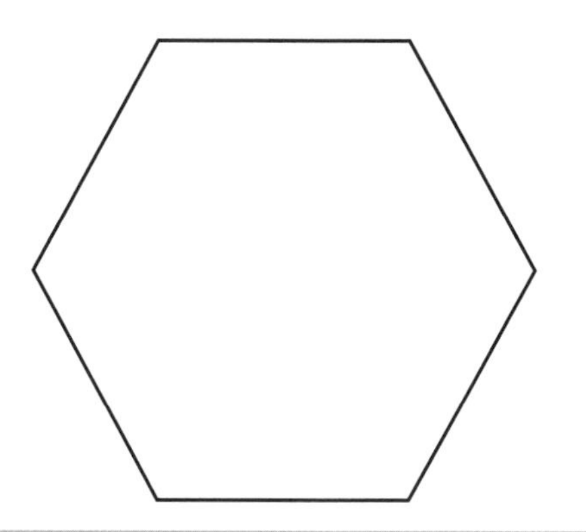

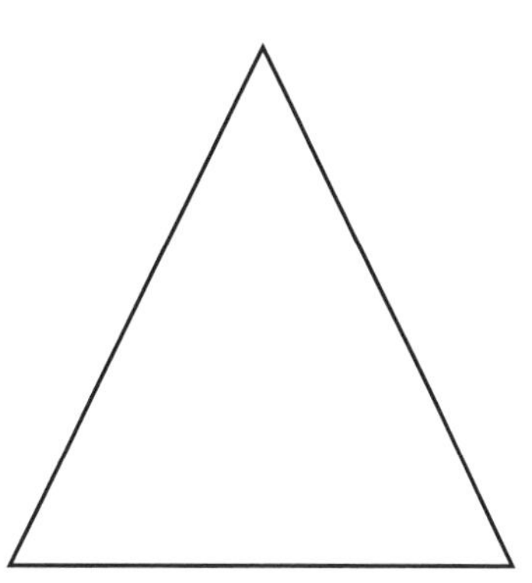

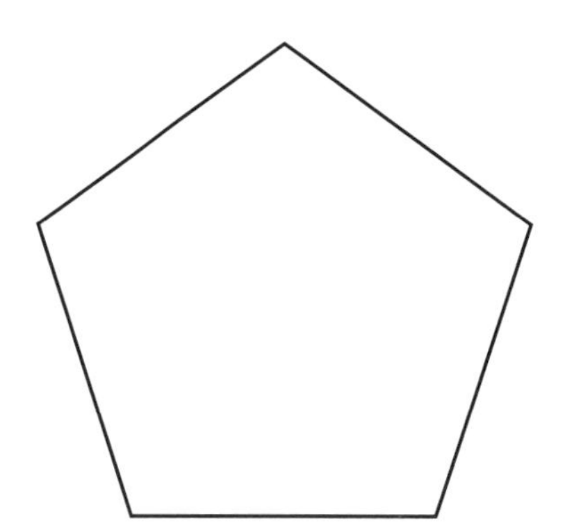

## 13 3D mystery shape

I am a 3D shape.

I have six edges.

I have four corners.

I have four triangular faces.

What is my name?

____________________

## 14 Time to reflect

On the right-hand side of the grid, draw the reflection of this pattern.

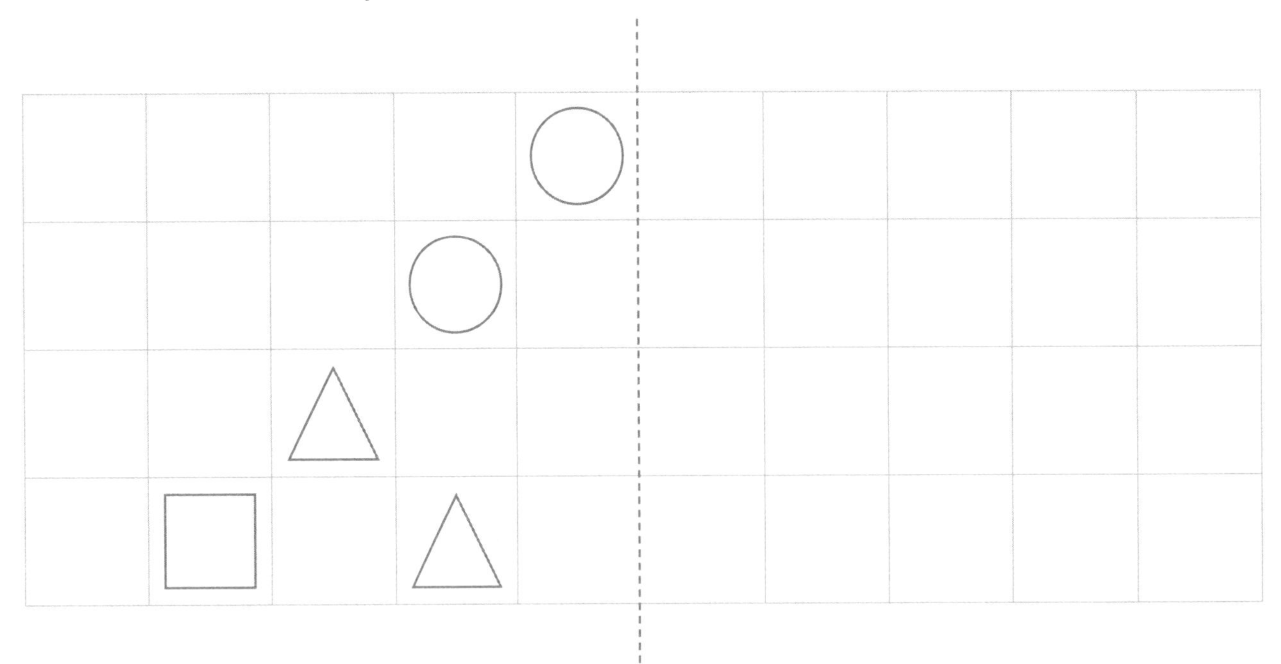

## 15 How tall?

Harry is taller than Barry and shorter than Gary.

Who is the tallest of the three?

______________________

## 16 Homemade jigsaw

Cut out two interesting pictures from a magazine. (Ask for permission first!)

Stick them onto two different pieces of card.

Cut them both into 20 pieces.

Shuffle all the pieces and see if you can put the two pictures back together again.

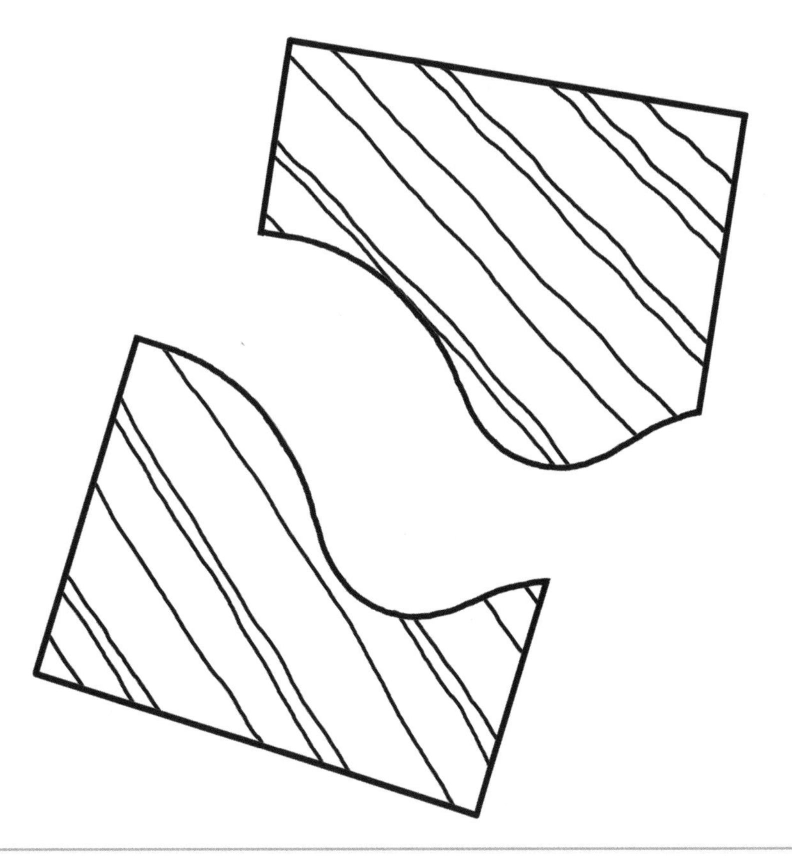

## 17 Stinky Stu

Stuart had a £2 coin.

He spent 82p on stink bombs!

How much change did he get?

£ ____________

## 18 Double up

I double the number 5,
then double the answer and
double that answer.

What number do I finish on?

## 19 Halve it

I halve the number 32, then halve the answer and halve that answer again

What number do I finish on?

## 20 Going bananas

Charlie the chubby chimp munched 10 bananas plus 11 bananas plus 12 bananas.

How many bananas did Charlie munch altogether?

## 21 Juggler

Dizzy the juggler juggled 14 eggs.

Dizzy slipped and dropped 5 of them!

How many eggs did Dizzy have left?

## 22 Multi-storey

There are five floors in this multi-storey car park.

There are seven cars parked on each floor.

How many cars are there in the car park in total?

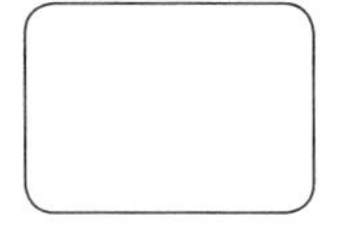

## 23 Generous Jenna

Generous Jenna is sharing out her gobstoppers.

She has 30 gobstoppers and shares them equally with five of her friends.

How many gobstoppers does each friend get?

## 24 Guess the weight

Which do you think is the most likely weight of:

- your Mum: 50g or 50kg?

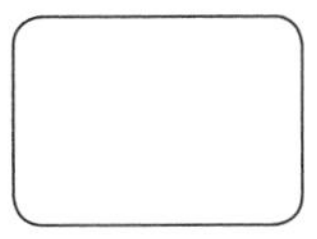

- a paperback book: 100kg or 100g?

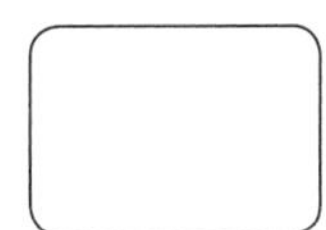

- a pet cat: 4kg or 40g?

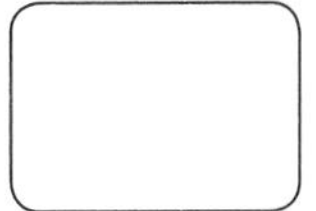

- a motorbike: 200kg or 2kg?

## 25 Balancing act

Kim and Jim are weighing themselves on a big set of scales.

16 bags of sand balance Kim.

15 bags of sand balance Jim.

How many bags of sand are needed to balance both of them together?

## 26 Thirsty work!

Martha the Elephant was thirsty, so she drank from her bucket.

How many litres of water did she leave in her bucket?

## 27 Coining it

Lorraine bought a bangle that cost 95p.

She used silver coins to pay for it.

Which coins could they have been?

Find at least five ways she could have paid for the bangle.

1 ______________________

2 ______________________

3 ______________________

4 ______________________

5 ______________________

## 28 Safe-cracker

Freddie Fingers the safe-cracker is at it again!

He needs to break the code to open the safe.

What are the next three numbers he needs to fill in?

Write them in the boxes.

88, 84, 80,

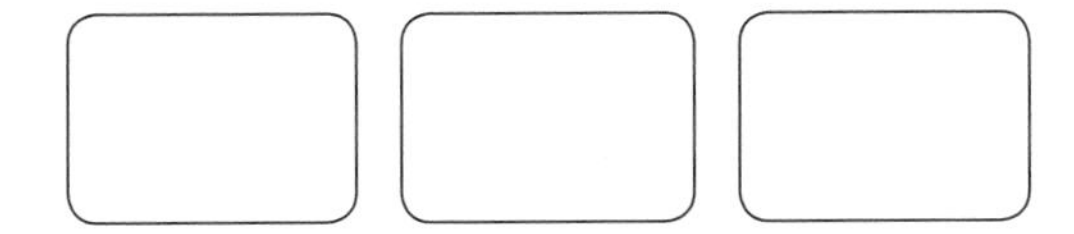

## 29 Shady shapes

Which of these shapes are half shaded?

## 30 Mixed-up Mickey

Poor Mickey keeps forgetting how to write his numbers in words and in digits.

Help him with the correct answers.

Write 173 in words.

______________________

______________________

______________________

Write 'one hundred and twenty-six' in digits.

## 31 Guess the amount

Guess how many pebbles there are in this jar.

An estimate is a good guess.

Write your estimate here.

Now count the pebbles.

How many pebbles are in the jar?

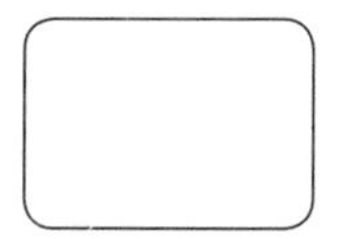

How close was your estimate?

## 32 Pairing-up challenge

Perfect Percy has found seven ways to make 100 using two numbers.

He has challenged you to find more! See if you can beat him.

Here is one to start you off:

60 + 40 = 100

## 33 Flower pots

Kasia has planted six flower seeds in each of these flower pots.

How many flowers will Kasia grow in total?

## 34 Who am I?

I am a flat shape.

I have three sides.

All my sides are equal in length.

What is my name?

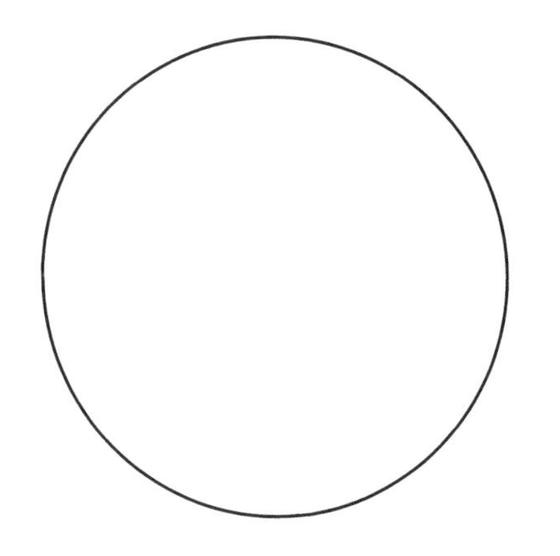

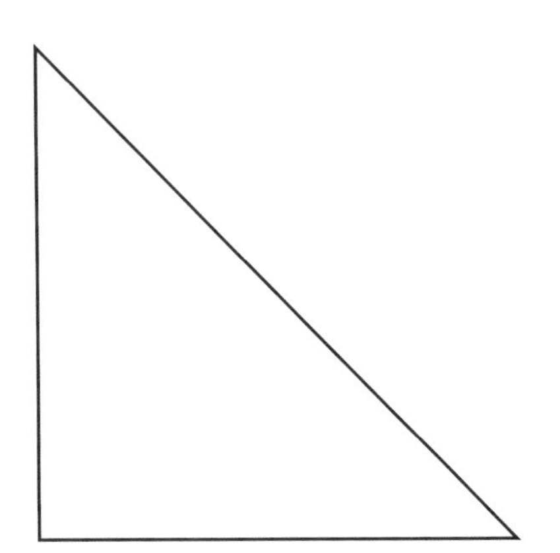

## 35 How long?

Estimate the lengths of these snakes.

Write your estimates here.

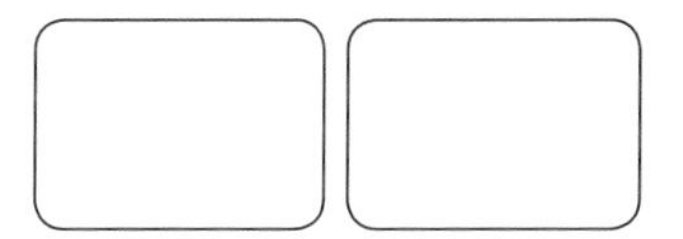

Now measure them with a ruler. How long are they?

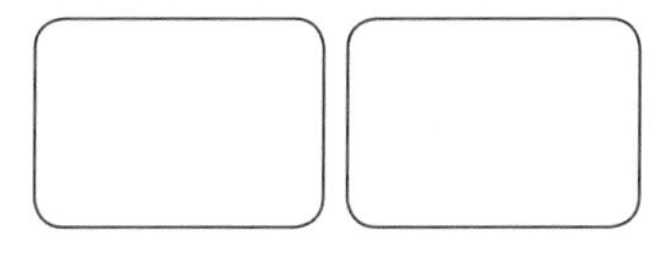

How close were your estimates?

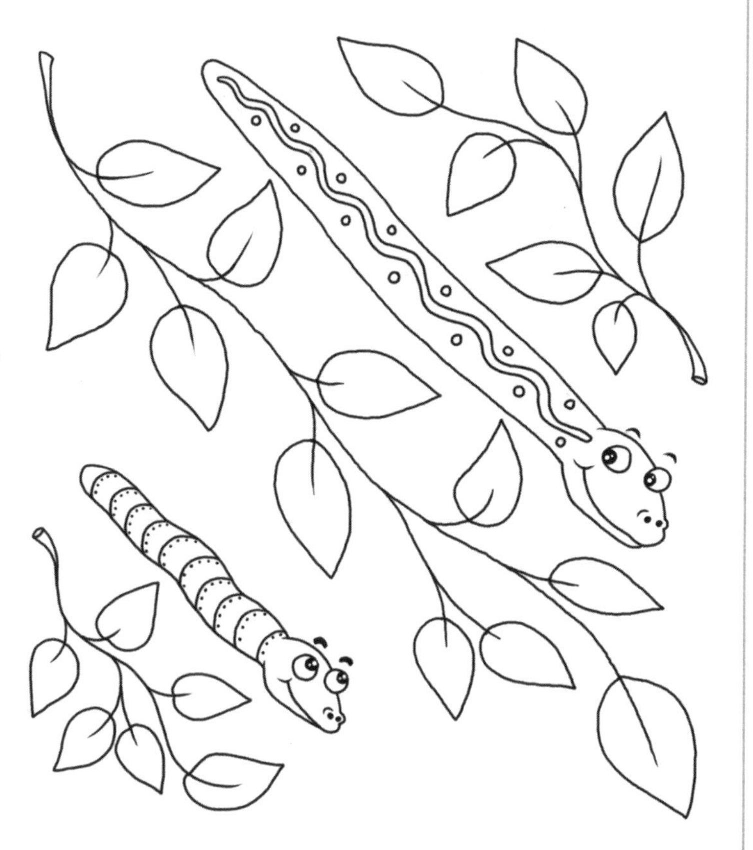

## 36 What would you use?

What would you use to measure the weight of this book?

What would you use to measure the length of this book?

## Block A

**P9** **Number line** Answers will vary.

**P10** **Combining cards** 16 possible answers: 11; 12; 15; 17; 31; 32; 35; 37; 41; 42; 45; 47; 71; 72; 75; 77.

**P11** **Dots before your eyes** 3 groups of 10 plus 3 = 33; 4 groups of 5 plus 4 = 24; 8 groups of 2 = 16.

**P12** **Fill your ladder** No answers.

**P13** **In the bin** No answers.

**P14** **Totals to 10** Answers will depend on numbers chosen by child.

**P15** **Stepping stones** Answers will depend on numbers chosen by teacher.

**P16** **Snaky stripes** Answers will depend on numbers chosen by teacher.

**P17** **Arrow sentences** Answers will depend on numbers chosen by teacher.

**P18** **Odds and evens** No answers.

**P19** **Opposites** No answers.

**P20** **Split the number** Answers will depend on numbers chosen by teacher.

## Block B

**P23** **Toy shopping** 11p = 10p + 1p; 30p = 20p + 10p; 21p = 20p + 1p; 32p = 20p + 10p + 2p; 26p = 20p + 5p + 1p; 28p = 20p + 5p + 2p + 1p; 33p = 20p + 10p + 2p + 1p; 42p = 20p + 20p + 2p. Other totals are possible using more coins.

**P24** **How much?** No answers.

**P25** **Describe me** **1** 6 sides, 6 corners, symmetrical, hexagon; **2** 8 sides, 8 corners, not symmetrical, octagon; **3** 5 sides, 5 corners, not symmetrical, pentagon; **4** 5 sides, 5 corners, symmetrical, pentagon; **5** 8 sides, 8 corners, symmetrical, octagon; **6** 6 sides, 6 corners, not symmetrical, hexagon.

**P26** **Double trouble maze**

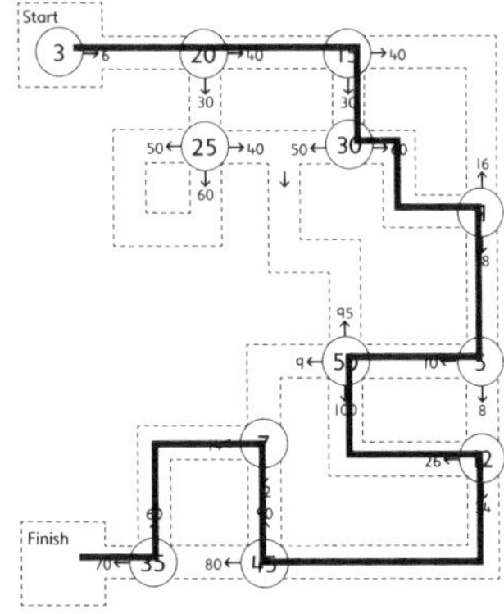


**P27** **Which coins?** Answers will depend on totals chosen by teacher.

**P28** **DJ Peejay** 3 × 5 = 15; 9 × 2 = 18; 4 × 10 = 40; 6 × 5 = 30; 7 × 2 = 14; 3 × 10 = 30; 8 × 5 = 40; 6 × 2 = 12; 7 × 10 = 70.

**P29** **The name game** 20 possible answers: 23; 24; 27; 28; 32; 34; 37; 38; 42; 43; 47; 48; 72; 73; 74; 78; 82; 83; 84; 87 (written as words and figures)

**P30** **Get some help!** Answers will vary.

**P31** **Beat the clock** 6 + **1** = 7; 5 + **2** = 7; 2 + **5** = 7; 4 + **3** = 7; 2 + **3** = 5; 0 + **5** = 5; 3 + **2** = 5; 5 + **0** = 5; **1** + 9 = 10; **7** + 3 = 10; **4** + 6 = 10; **8** + 2 = 10; 9 – **2** = 7; 10 – **3** = 7; 10 – **4** = 6; 8 – **1** = 7; 7 – **2** = 5; 8 – **3** = 5; 9 – **4** = 5; 5 – **0** = 5; **9** – 9 = 0; **8** – 3 = 5; **10** – 6 = 4; **9** – 2 = 7.

**P32** **Shape puzzle** Answers will depend on numbers chosen by teacher.

**P33** **Give us a clue!** Square; triangle; cylinder; circle or cone; sphere; cube or cuboid; cone; cube or cuboid.

**P34** **Reflective symmetry** I, E, O, Y, M and T have lines of symmetry. (O and I each have two lines of symmetry.)

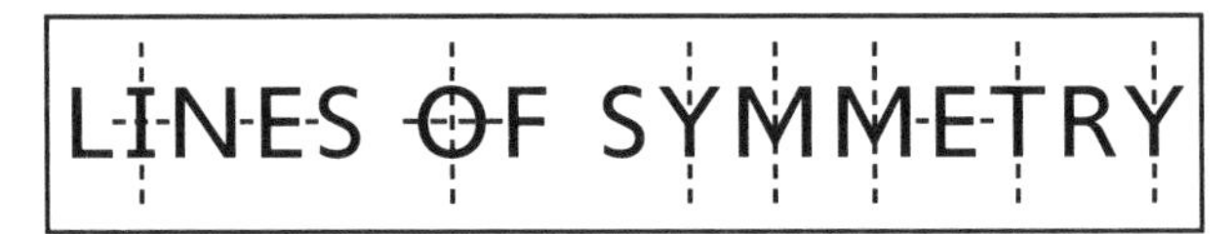


**P35** **Rounding up** Answers will vary.

**P36** **Making problems** Answers will vary.

**P37** **Right or wrong?** **1** right; **2** right; **3** wrong (there are more than three possible ways).

**P38** **What a problem!** Answers will depend on numbers chosen by teacher.

**P39** **Doubles and halves** Answers will depend on numbers chosen by teacher.

**P40** **You are the teacher!** Jimmy: **1** ✗; **2** ✗; **3** ✓; **4** ✓; **5** ✗; Total 2/5. Grace: **1** ✗; **2** ✓; **3** ✓; **4** ✗; **5** ✓; Total 3/5.

## Block C

**P43** **Measures** String 12cm; apples exactly 2kg; bananas just over 4kg; liquid (left) just over 2 litres; liquid (right) just under 1 litre.

**P44** **Reading scales** 10cm; 3.5kg; 1 litre.

**P45** **Sorting it out** Yellow, white and red are the three most popular colours.

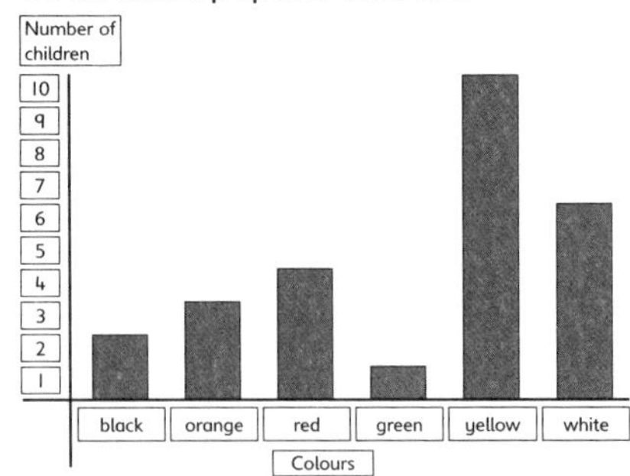


**P46** **How long is it?** Answers will vary.

**P47** **Favourite colours** Answers will vary.

**P48** **Faulty graph** Possible errors include: No zero on vertical axis; no 4 on vertical axis; each axis label is wrong – they need to be swapped over (2 faults); 'Cow' column not sitting on horizontal axis; wrong title (it is a block graph, not a pictogram); wrong number of hens shown on graph.

**P49 Sort it out!**

**P50 Slippery Sid** 6cm, 9cm, 11cm, 13cm and 14cm.

**P51 Measure it** Ribbon 23cm; bananas 5kg; oranges: just over 4.5kg; liquid (left) 1.5 litres; liquid (right) 2 litres.

**P52 Draw the measures** Check the arrows are accurately drawn.

**P53 Animal information**

| | Lions | Tigers | Crocodiles | Gorillas | Bears | Spiders |
|---|---|---|---|---|---|---|
| No. of children | 7 | 8 | 2 | 5 | 3 | 1 |

**1** Tiger; **2** Spider; **3** 26 children.

**P54 Tasty take-aways**

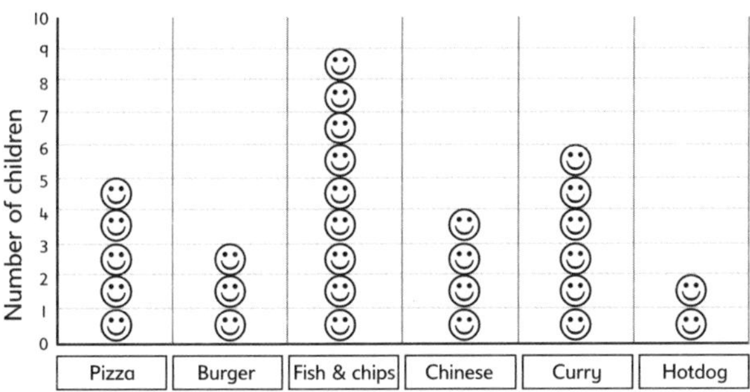


## Block D

**P57 Time for snap!** No answers.

**P58 Which method?** Answers will depend on calculations chosen by teacher.

**P59 Pence to pounds** 175p = £1.75; 345p = £3.45; 225p = £2.25; 269p = £2.69; 180p = £1.80; 199p = £1.99; 130p = £1.30; 150p = £1.50; 150p = £1.50; 120p = £1.20; 155p = £1.55; 150p = £1.50.

**P60 Nature trail** leaf 26cm; log 3kg; water in jug 150ml; centipede 4cm; rock 100g; tea in jug (next to flask) 200ml.

**P61 Telling the time**

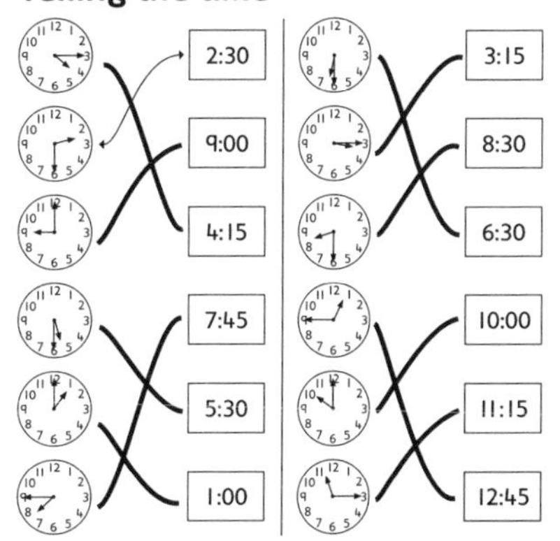


**P62 Where is the arrow?** Above; clockwise; anticlockwise; below; behind; in front; beside; quarter turn; right angle.

**P63 Position, direction or movement?** *Position words:* under; corner; outside; right; higher; lower; front; back; beside; middle; left. *Direction words:* clockwise; anticlockwise; towards; backwards; across; sideways. *Movement words:* slide; quarter turn; right angle; straight line; roll.

**P64 Robo-dog** One possible solution is: Move 5 squares forward; make a quarter turn clockwise; move 3 squares forward – reach/rescue girl – move 1 square forward; make a quarter turn anticlockwise; move 2 squares forward; make a quarter turn clockwise; move 3 squares forward – rescue man – make a quarter turn clockwise; move 3 squares forward; make a quarter turn clockwise; move 1 square forward; make a quarter turn anticlockwise; move 2 squares forward; make a quarter turn clockwise; move 1 square forward – rescue boy – make a quarter turn anticlockwise; move 1 square forward; make a quarter turn clockwise; move 5 squares forward; make a quarter turn anticlockwise; move 1 square forward – arrive back at tunnel entrance.

**P65 Time crossword** *Across:* **2** morning; **4** after; **5** afternoon; **7** early; **9** late; **10** evenings; **11** digital. *Down:* **1** fortnight; **3** watch; **4** analogue; **6** seconds; **8** minute.

**P66 Can you find my partner?** No answers.

**P67 Match the time** No answers.

**P68 How fast?** **1** 10km/h; **2** 20km/h; **3** 15km/h; **4** 12km/h; **5** 18km/h; **6** 21km/h; **7** 23km/h; **8** 4km/h.

## Block E

**P71 Loopy lines** Answers will depend on multiplications or divisions chosen by teacher.

**P72 Quarter mastery** The cross, hexagon and double-headed arrow can be quartered; the pentagon, heart and triangle cannot be quartered.

**P73 Percy's hungry** No answers.

**P74 Investigate these facts** Answers will depend on numbers chosen by teacher.

**P75 Bridging 10** No answers.

**P76 Equivalents**

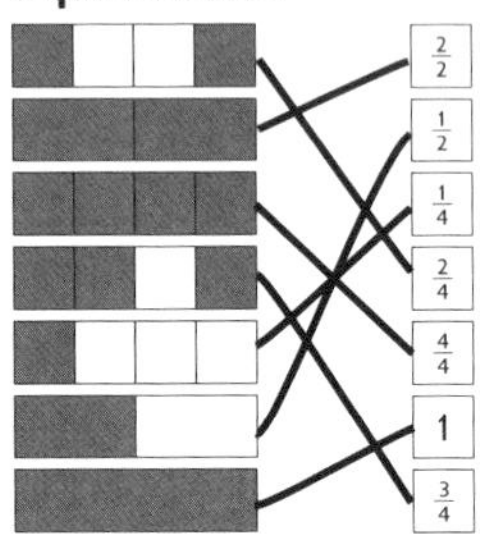

½ = ¼ + ¼; 1 whole = ½ +½ or ¼ + ¾;
¾ = ¼ + ½.

**P77 Spotting multiples** *Multiples of 2:* 2, 4, 6, 8, 10, 12, 14, 16, 18, 20
*Multiples of 5:* 10,15, 20, 25
*Multiples of 10:* 10, 20
*Multiples of 2:* 32, 34, 36, 38, 40, 42, 44, 46, 48, 50 *and 5:* 35, 40, 45, 50
*Multiples of 5:* 50, 55, 60 *and 10:* 50, 60
*Multiples of 2:* 44, 12, 78, 14, 16, 60, 38.
All even numbers are multiples of 2.

**P78 Spider charts** No answers.

**P79 All the same value** Multiples of 10p up to 60p (ie the toys could cost 10p, 20p, 30p, 40p, 50p or 60p each); multiples of 5p up to 30p (ie the toys could cost 5p, 10p, 15p, 20p, 25p or 30p each).

**P80 Grouping** Answers will depend on numbers chosen by teacher.

**P81 Halves and quarters** Answers will vary.

**P82 Mixed bag of problems** **1** 3 black kittens; **2** 9 chocolates; **3** 4 boxes; **4** £5.75; **5** ten 10p coins; **6** 38p; **7** £40.

**P83 How many ways?** Answers will depend on numbers chosen by teacher.

**P84 Fraction problems** Answers will depend on numbers chosen by teacher.

**P85 What's the difference between...?** **1** 6; **2** 14; **3** 9; **4** 28; **5** 9; **6** 19; **7** 38; **8** 18.

**P86 Magic Mike** 26 – 12 = **14**; 31 – **18** = 13; **44** – 20 = 24; 17 – **4** = 13; **37** – 23 = 14; **48** – 37 = 11; 36 – **12** = 24; 29 – 17 = **12**.

**P87 Dartboards**

**P88 Friendly number quiz** **1** 25; **2** 40; **3** 16; **4** 45; **5** 70; **6** 12; **7** 5; **8** 5; **9** 6; **10** 28; **11** 45; **12** 30.

## Puzzles and problems answers

1 **Comics** 20p; 10p + 10p; 10p + 5p + 5p; 5p + 5p + 5p + 5p

2 **Unlucky Ducky** 6 + 5 + 2; 6 + 4 + 3; 6 + 4 + 2 + 1 (three ways)

3 **Santa's little helper** 5, 5 and 5; 5, 4 and 6; 5, 3 and 7; 5, 2 and 8; 5, 1 and 9 (five ways)

4 **Hopscotch**

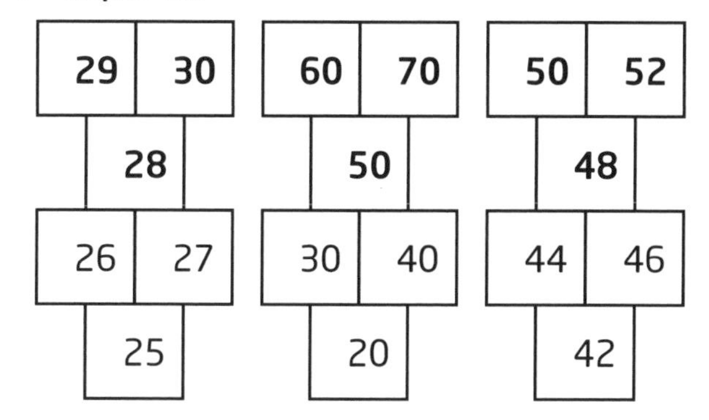


5 **Puzzling pyramid** 9 triangles

6 **Let's play darts!** Highest possible score 21 (7, 7, 7); other possible scores are 15 (4, 5, 6); 16 (4, 5, 7); 17 (4, 6, 7); 18 (5, 6, 7)

7 **How long?** Snake **1** 6cm; Snake **2** 9cm

8 **That's dicey!** Six (1, 5, 6; 2, 4, 6; 3, 3, 6; 5, 2, 5; 5, 3, 4; 4, 4, 4)

9 **Take your seats!** 7, 18, 25, 33, 41, 59, 67, 73, 80, 92

10 **Where am I heading?** West

11 **Is that the time?** 8.30pm

12 **2D mystery shape** A rectangle

13 **3D mystery shape** Triangular-based pyramid

14 **Time to reflect**

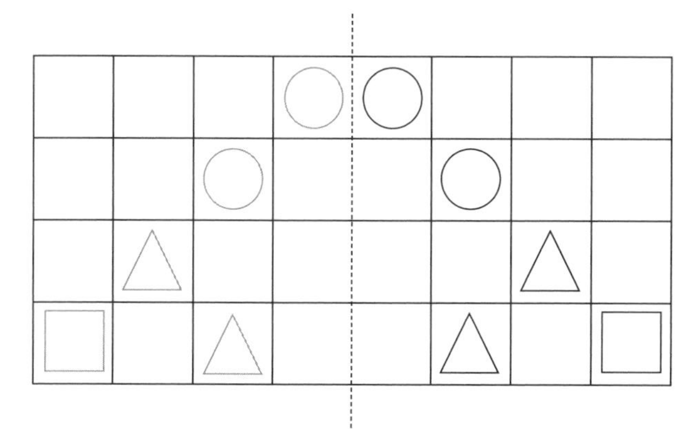

15 **How tall?** Gary

16 **Homemade jigsaw** Children make their own jigsaws

17 **Stinky Stu** £1.18

18 **Double up** 40

19 **Halve it** 4

20 **Going bananas** 33 bananas

21 **Juggler** 9 eggs

22 **Multi-storey** 35 cars

23 **Generous Jenna** 6

24 **Guess the weight** Mum 50kg; cat 4kg; paperback book 100g; motorbike 200kg

25 **Balancing act** 31 bags of sand

26 **Thirsty work!** 6 litres

27 **Coining it** Five possible answers:
50p + 20p + 20p + 5p;
50p + 20p + 10p + 10p + 5p;
50p + 20p + 10p + 5p + 5p + 5p;
50p + 10p + 10p + 10p + 10p + 5p;
20p + 20p + 20p + 20p + 10p + 5p

28 **Safe-cracker** 76, 72, 68

29 **Shady shapes**

30 **Mixed-up Mickey** One hundred and seventy-three; 126

31 **Guess the amount** Estimates will vary; 27

32 **Pairing-up challenge** Possible answers include: 90 + 10; 80 + 20; 70 + 30; 60 + 40; 50 + 50; 75 + 25; 99 + 1; 87 + 13; and there are many more!

33 **Flower pots** 36 flowers

34 **Who am I?** Equilateral triangle

35 **How long?** Estimates will vary; 5cm, 9cm

36 **What would you use?** Scales; a ruler

## Also available in this series:

ISBN 978-1407-10216-0

ISBN 978-1407-10217-7

ISBN 978-1407-10218-4

ISBN 978-1407-10219-1

ISBN 978-1407-10220-7

ISBN 978-1407-10221-4

To find out more, call: 0845 603 9091
or visit our website www.scholastic.co.uk